# The
# Trans-Siberian
# Express

# The Trans-Siberian Express

by

*V. Kuranov*

translated by

**Anatol Kagan**

SPHINX PRESS, INC.
New York

Library of Congress Cataloging in Publication Data

Kuranov, V
    The Trans-Siberian Express.

    Translation of Strela cherez Sibif.
    Includes index.
    1.   Siberia—Description and travel—1945-
2.   Trans-Siberian Railroad.
DK756.K8313            915.7            79-3106
ISBN 0-8236-8651-5

*Place-name spellings in this book conform generally to the transliteration system approved by the Board on Geographic Names, U.S. Department of the Interior.*

# Contents

of Siberia and the Far East / Table 4: Production of Timber / Table 5: Production of Oil and Natural Gas in Siberia / Table 6: Largest Rivers of Siberia and the Far East / Table 7: Number of Physicians in Siberia and the Far East

# List of Photographs

# V. Kuranov

The Trans-Siberian Express

# Introduction

The great Trans-Siberian Railroad, the largest railroad in the world (9,300 kilometers), was built at the end of the nineteenth and the beginning of the twentieth centuries. It was written in European papers at the time that the construction of the Great Siberian Line would have the same significance for the progress of civilization as the building of the Suez Canal had had.

The journey by the *Russia* express on this railroad which links Moscow with Vladivostok, a major Soviet port on the coast of the Pacific Ocean, is an interesting and gripping experience. The train passes through or close to 120 cities and towns. Each place represents a page out of ancient Russian history, as well as the present and future of the Soviet State.

Zagorsk, Yaroslavl, and Rostov marked the beginning of the Russian State. The Ural cities and towns arose on the sites where, in accordance with the orders of Peter the Great, the first iron works were established. Irkutsk and Tobolsk marked the beginning of the conquest of Siberia. Sverdlovsk, Omsk, and Komsomolsk-on-the-Amur were the first industrial bastions of the young Socialist Russia, created in the thirties. Bratsk, Angarsk, and Ust-Ilimsk are the new Siberia, the harbingers of its future.

What do you, the reader, know about Siberia, about the vast austere land east of Moscow and beyond the Ural Mountains? It is possible that you may have read about Siberian gold and have seen Siberian furs. But do you know that half of the world's coal deposits and one-third of the forest wealth of the globe are concentrated in Siberia? Much is written about Siberia these days, and each year more and more economists, journalists, social scientists, politicians and businessmen, people trying to forecast future international developments, come to the same conclusion: only he who knows Siberia, its present life and its future prospects, can talk seriously about the future of the world.

It is impossible not to wonder at the limitless Siberian *taiga*,[1] or at Lake Baykal, unique and mysterious in its own way; and surely there isn't anyone who could contemplate the majestic Amur River with indifference.

And yet, it is not the amazing beauties of nature which astound the traveler in Russia but the striking evidence of the self-denying love of the Soviet people, who have transformed the vast spaces from the Carpathian Mountains to the Pacific coast and Sakhalin. This is particularly noticeable in Siberia where neither the frosts of −50° Celsius nor the unbearable heat halts the work of construction in the great renewal of the land. Young people travel to Siberia to build with their own hands.

The *Russia* express travels from Moscow to Vladivostok in a week—170 hours. It flies like an arrow from

---

[1] The vast, swampy, coniferous forest region of Siberia.

west to east, crossing seven time zones and traveling through regions that vary in climate, flora, and fauna, as well as in national and socioeconomic characteristics. Each section of the journey provides new impressions, ample food for thought, and considerable satisfaction.

It is hoped that before you make your reservation on the Trans-Siberian express, you will start your journey with this book.

# Part I

# The First Thousand Kilometers

## Moscow —Komsomol Square

Our journey begins from Komsomol Square, often called the square of the three stations. At different times, steel links were established from here: with Leningrad, with Central Asia, and with the Far East.

The square was named in honor of the Moscow Komsomoltsy[2] who, in the years of the stormy construction of the foundation of Socialist industry, used to depart from these three stations to faraway lands to build mills, factories, hydroelectric stations, railroads, and seaports.

The oldest of the stations—the Leningrad—was built in the middle of the last century in late classical style and recalls the wonderful architecture of Russia's former capital, St. Petersburg (now Leningrad).[3] The

[2] Members of the Young Communist League.
[3] St. Petersburg became Petrograd in 1914 and Leningrad in 1924, upon Lenin's death.

first two-track railroad of Russia linked St. Petersburg and Moscow in 1851.

Across the square, opposite the Leningrad Station, there is another—the Kazan Station. It is the most original building on the square, and from it, connection by rail with Kazan, 900 kilometers east of Moscow, was opened at the end of the last century. A multistory tower reminiscent of the tower of the Kazan Kremlin and crowned by a tall spire with the biggest weathervane in the country commands attention. The building is also adorned by an original clock which displays a blue face and the signs of the zodiac. From the Kazan Station the railroad goes to the Republics of Central Asia, Kazakhstan, and Southern Siberia.

Trains for Vladivostok leave from the Yaroslavl Station, which stands beside the Leningrad Station. Erected in 1904 from the design of the architect F. Shekhtel, the building was styled in the spirit of ancient Russian architecture, with a characteristic pitched timbered roof surmounted by traditional fretwork decorations. The station does not appear large, but it is very spacious. When it was reconstructed 12 years ago, the facade was left untouched while the waiting rooms were considerably enlarged.

Looking through the huge windows of the two-story building of the Yaroslavl Station, you can see an endless stream of people proceeding to the long-distance and suburban trains. Conversation in different languages flows unceasingly here, day or night. Passengers at Yaroslavl Station differ from passengers elsewhere. They are more particular, unhurried in a characteristic Siberian way, and usually burdened with a considerable amount of luggage. This is understandable, for an inhabitant of Siberia does not often travel for thousands of kilometers to Moscow. And then it is necessary for the traveler to bring back to all his relatives and acquaintances a memorable gift from the capital.

The journey ahead will be long. For this reason, the assembly of passenger coaches of the Trans-Siberian Railroad represents 14-16 one-story houses on wheels, equipped according to up-to-date world standards.

The *Russia* express has pulled in to the platform. The dark red coaches have just left a refreshing shower and gleam with ruby drops. In half an hour, the train's departure will be announced over its public address system, visitors seeing people off will leave the compartments, and the train will start smoothly—without a whistle (sound signals are prohibited in Moscow). It will gather speed, and villages on the fringes of Moscow will flash past the windows. The wind will evaporate the drops, the coaches will darken, and finally, when the train breaks from among the surrounding houses and industrial buildings, it will fly through an avenue of endless forest which adjoins Moscow and which gradually merges with the gardens and parks of the city.

# Zagorsk—Treasury of Antiquities

The deep horn of the powerful electric locomotive pulling the coaches of *Russia* is lost and then echoes back in the tunnel formed by the eternally silent conifers; large and small bridges rumble beneath the wheels. Passengers involuntarily fall silent as they grow accustomed to the speed. *Russia* races from Moscow to Vladivostok, leaving behind hot windgusts, humming rails, and the smell of metal and engine oil.

But only casual passers-by near the train track notice the speed. The passengers soon become used to the swift passage of trees, suburban platforms, and kilometer posts outside the windows. Only faint echoes of the roar of the steel bridges left behind reach the people within the all-metal coaches. Well-insulated from the outside world, they become acquainted with their fellow travelers, exchanging opinions on the weather, the international situation and much, much else. . . Suddenly a train moving in the opposite direction rushes past, a gust of wind whips up the window curtain, and for a moment, the air in the compartment presses against the eardrums. Only during this moment do the passengers feel the speed again.

*Russia* does not stop at Zagorsk, 60 kilometers from Moscow, but the travelers are told over the public address system that Zagorsk is the site of the Troïtse-Sergiyeva Lavra, a monastery famous thoughout the country. It was founded in the depth of the forest by the monk Sergius in the middle of the fourteenth century at a time when the tribute to be paid to the Tartars lay like a heavy burden on the shoulders of the Russian people. The monastery played an important part in the unification of ancient Russia, which was split up into principalities, and in its liberation from the Tartar yoke. Later on, it became the center of hand-written literature. In the fifteenth century the monks copied books by hand, adorned them with vignettes, with gold and vermillion letters, and with miniatures. The "sergiyevskiy" style of writing books was highly valued. The monastery also had a very large library where the rarest manuscripts were kept.

In the decade 1540-1550, impregnable stone fortress walls and 10 defense towers were erected around the Troïtse-Sergiyeva Lavra. They protected Moscow from invaders from the northeast.

At the beginning of 1689 the future reorganizer of Russia, Czar Peter the Great, who feared the crafty intrigues of his political opponents, fled to the shelter of the Lavra's powerful walls. From here, he began the struggle for a strong unified Russia.

Today, everything in the Troïtse-Sergiyeva Lavra is preserved as it was hundreds of years ago. It has become a museum sanctuary where priceless treasures can be seen: ancient books, artistic works of gold and silver, and old church implements. Visitors stop for a long time in front of the ikons of such famous Russian masters as Andrei Roublyov and Danila Cherny (fifteenth century) and Simon Oushakov (seventeenth century). Paul of Aleppo, a seventeenth-century traveler from Siberia, wrote of the Zagorsk monastery: "This monastery has no equal either in the land of Muskovy or anywhere else in the world." And Russian ikon painters, according to Paul, "have no equal in the world in their art, refinement and professional skill . . .The human mind cannot grasp their essence and appraise their outstanding performance."

The architectural complex of the monastery comprises the Troïtskiy and Zvenigorodskiy Cathedrals (fifteenth century), the Dukhovskaya Church, the stone cells of the monks (called the Predtechenskiy Block), the refectory, and the bell tower. Here, also, is the burial vault of the Russian Czar Boris Godunov (beginning of the seventeenth century) and of the members of his family.

The Orthodox Theological Academy is located here, and services continue as before in these churches which are outstanding for their sumptuous decoration and the beauty of their architectural forms.

Past Zagorsk, villages and stations appear less and less frequently, and the eye skips along the tops of bluish pine woods. From here to Vladivostok there are brief stops every 100-300 kilometers. Longer stops of 15 to 20 minutes are only provided in the major cities, where the electric locomotive leaves for the depot and is replaced by another.

# The Great Siberian Railroad Is 75 Years Old

There were many proposals for a Trans-Siberian Railroad. The first ones go back to 1875. It was suggested, for example, that an "Amur Company" be organized to construct a rail link between Irkutsk and Chita. Another project visualized the construction of a railroad with traction by horse right up to the Pacific Ocean. All of these proposals, some of them absolutely unrealistic, were discussed by the Russian press and the public. Siberian industrialists and traders demanded a railroad most insistently. They even applied by letter to the Czar: "Only us, Thy children, O Emperor, are far from Thee, if not in heart, then in space. We suffer great hardship from this. . . . Grant us the railroad, bring us close to Thee."

A railroad was also needed by the Siberian peasants, who had to dispose of grain, meat, and furs. Villages lost in the limitless steppes and forests beyond the Urals traded in "natural" products and dreamed of exchanging their goods for beautiful "town" wares, fabrics, machines, agricultural implements, and metal products.

Perhaps the only opponents of the railroad were the coachmen. Sixteen thousand coachmen and 80,000 horses, harnessed to sleighs, carts, and coaches, transported—on only one section between Tomsk and Irkutsk—50,000 tons of cargo and masses of passengers every year. Hundreds of thousands of horses sped daily in different directions, in the Urals, in Siberia, in the Far East, carrying out the work which should have been undertaken by the Trans-Siberian Railroad.

The construction of the line beyond the Ural mountain range commenced, to all intents and purposes, in 1892. Engaged in its construction were peasant teams, townspeople, military construction units, and Siberian prisoners. The basic building "machines" were spades, wheelbarrows, and horse-drawn carts. Only later, did American excavating equipment start to appear here and there. Thousands upon thousands of people worked daily on the construction of the railroad bed. Each kilometer of the line was amply drenched with human sweat and blood. The builders had to overcome forest growth hundreds of years old, swamps, and precipitous mountains. They also encountered a phenomenon hitherto unknown to railroad builders: permafrost. The fact is that the ground in most districts of Siberia is always frozen. However, the top layer melts in summer, and sometimes it turns into a liquid mass which carries away the structures put up during winter.

Nevertheless, permanent traffic beyond the Urals was opened on the West Siberian section of the line in the fourth year of building. Three years later, trains went as far as Lake Baykal and the construction crossed to the other bank of the lake. The trains used to be taken across the lake on a huge ferry-icebreaker, the *Baykal*, which could carry 28 loaded cars and 670 passengers. In 1904, however, traffic began to move over the whole length of the line; by 1905, special terraces for the railroad bed were successfully cut into the rocky shore and dozens of tunnels were drilled through the unapproachable rocks. Trains started to operate on the Krugobaykalskaya Railroad bordering this magnificent lake.

The longest railroad in the world, the Trans-Siberian Line transformed Siberia and the Far East. The landless peasants of European Russia streamed into the free regions beyond the Urals. More than 4 million people from European Russia settled in Siberia from 1895 to 1914. The population figure beyond the Urals doubled. The settlers cleared the taiga, built solid houses, and plowed the land. Most peasant households had two houses, one for the winter where the family lived permamently, and the other some distance away, for the summer, situated on the so-called *zaïmka*—free land for mowing and plowing, to which the peasant could drive. The grain yield was relatively low here due to the harsh climate, and therefore the settlers sowed as much land as possible.

Foreign businessmen also streamed into Siberia. Headquarters of international capital were established in

Omsk, and the consular flags of Denmark, Sweden, Great Britain, Germany and the United States began to appear in the streets.

The British conducted gold mining operations in the Lena gold fields and extracted copper from the Mariinskiy mines. Scandinavian and German businessmen bought up Siberian butter in cedar barrels, Siberian furs, and sheep's wool from the peasants. Lumber, lignite, non-ferrous metals, coal, and salt were sent abroad. By 1917, foreign investments in the Siberian economy exceeded 258 million roubles. The Russian journal *Siberian Questions* remarked with bitterness: "Foreign capital in Siberia considers itself as a European who, for the time being, has established trading posts among savages, who legally own huge natural resources."

The number of towns along the railroad increased from 40 to 63 between 1897 and 1917. They arose at mining sites and railroad workshops. The native Siberian population began to migrate from villages to cities closer to the railroad. At the same time, the population figures of the old Siberian towns increased three to five times.

Inhuman exploitation of the workers by Russian and foreign capital led inevitably to a growth of self-consciousness and revolutionary activity among the toilers. The most memorable action was the strike at the Lena gold fields in March, 1912. At first the strike had a peaceful and organized character. But the Czarist government, at the demand of the British owners, issued orders for a cruel showdown with the strikers. The police arrested the strike committee. In response, nearly 3,000 workers marched to the administration building to hand the state attorney a complaint against the authorities' illegal action and a request for the release of those arrested. The workers' procession was met by rifle volleys from the troops: 270 workers were killed and 250 were wounded.

The executioners did not succeed in breaking the will of the strikers. As a sign of protest, the workers and their families left the gold fields.

The drama on the Lena called forth a storm of protest throughout the whole of Russia. A wave of strikes in sympathy with the Siberian people swept the country. Lenin, the leader and organizer of the October Revolution of 1917, wrote: "The Lena shooting was the cause for the transformation of the revolutionary mood of the masses into the revolutionary uprising of the masses."

## Rostov and Yaroslavl: At the Origins of the Russian State

But let us return to our express train, *Russia*, speeding north from Zagorsk across the ancient territory of Rostov and Souzdal.

History bestowed on Rostov the name Rostov the Great, although it is smaller than the neighboring Yaroslavl and smaller even than Zagorsk. It is situated on the shores of the vast, picturesque, but comparatively shallow Lake Nero. The town's industry is not extensive: a flax-spinning mill and a molasses factory.

However, this district center of the Yaroslav region alone is visited yearly by thousands of tourists from all parts of the Soviet Union and from abroad.

Rostov is one of the oldest towns in the country, much older than Moscow. During the ninth and tenth centuries, Rostov was already an important center of ancient Russia in the northeast. Through it passed the trade routes to the Volga. During the eleventh century it became the principal town of the Rostov-Souzdal principality and later of the Rostov principality. The chronicles speak of the might and wealth of the Rostov princes and bishops and of the priceless relics of Russian culture collected in their treasuries. The library of Prince Constantine, which contained a large number of the rarest manuscripts, was particularly famous. Unfortunately, this library perished in the thirteenth century, during the Tartar-Mongol invasion.

The town did not have the means to reconstruct what had been destroyed during successive invasions by nomads and the armed bands of the princes. It was languishing. At one time, not only its land but the town itself was divided up among the princes. A saying has been preserved in the Russian language since those days: "In the Rostov country there is a prince in every village." By the end of the fifteenth century, Rostov had been annexed by Moscow.

The passing ages have not preserved much of the cultural heritage of Rostov the Great, but that which has survived is sufficient to make us admire the distinctive beauty and elegance of the manufactured articles and the refined taste of the ancient Russian craftsmen. Today, the central part of the town, the Rostov Kremlin, is converted to a museum of its own kind of ancient architecture.

From whichever road the traveler approaches Rostov, he sees white-walled churches and buildings of fairy-tale beauty across the treeless land, from as far away as

10 kilometers. Many visitors remark on the harmony and orderliness of the architectural panorama of Rostov. Its impact, penetrating deeply into the soul, can be compared with a festive grand melody performed by an orchestra of a thousand players. Above the town, above the blue expanse of Lake Nero rises the Kremlin, and on its outskirts, the Avramiyevskiy and Spasso-Yakovlevskiy monastaries. The viewer is charmed by a variety on sharply pinnacled watchtowers and rotund, large and small church bells, by the whiteness of the fortress walls and the gleaming of the gilded church domes.

In the center of the Kremlin, the Church of the Savior, with a high-pitched roof and a golden dome, commands the entrance. Next stands the Church of John the Divine, somewhat further on, the White Hall which Peter the Great used to visit, and finally the bulk of the Ouspenskiy Cathedral. Bishops and princes were buried within it, as in all cathedrals of Russian principalities and bishoprics. A place of honor is accorded the tomb of the builder of the Rostov Kremlin, Yona Sysoyevich.

Ancient ikons, frescoes, artwork made of precious metals, and artistically shaped objects of the past are exhibited in the museums of the Kremlin. Of interest to the lover of pictorial and sculptural art are the church wall paintings and some of the sepulchres, for example, the stone cross above the grave of the son of the deacon Stephan Borodatyy (fifteenth century). The bas reliefs amaze by the softness and harmony of their lines. The slightly stooped figures personify sorrow without affectation and contrived drama.

The scientist-restorers continue the work of examination and restoration of the Kremlin and other monuments of Rostov for which the Soviet government has allocated the necessary means. Every year, more of the creations of Russia's ancient architects rise from the ruins brought about by time.

In the sixteenth and seventeenth centuries, the Rostov art of building exerted a strong influence on the work of the masters engaged in Yaroslavl, where the *Russia* express will stop.

The town of Yaroslavl, founded in 1024 by Prince Yaroslav the Wise, did not play as large a part in the development of the Russian State as Rostov did. Only for a short time was it the capital of the Yaroslav principality, forming at times part of the Rostov-Souzdal principality and at other times, of Muskovy.

Yaroslavl developed and grew much faster than Rostov. Situated on the Volga River, at the mouth of the Kotorosl River, it occupied a favorable position along the trade routes: through it passed both the river and land route from Moscow to the north. The inhabitants of the town and the surroundings, who speak the Volga dialect of the Russian language have always been famed for enterprise, speed, and decisiveness in their actions. In the past, they were also marked by a high level of education, compared with that of the almost universally illiterate Russia. The actor Fyodor Volkov founded the first Russian professional theatre in Yaroslavl, in 1750. It was in Yaroslavl that *Uyedinyony Poshekhonets*[4] appeared, the first journal to be published in an outlying area. And Yaroslavl was one of the first towns in Russia to establish a school of advanced science.

[4] *The Solitary Simpleton*

At present, Yaroslavl is a large industrial city with a population of 584,000 people; it is a regional center, a railway junction, and a river port. Machine building, metallurgy, and chemical and rubber-asbestos industries have been established in Soviet times. Hydro- and thermoelectric stations have been erected, as well as automobile plants and oil refineries, a polygraphic complex, and food production enterprises. Yaroslavl has its own television station, newspapers, several institutes of higher education, more than 130 libraries, and approximately 80 schools.

The first woman cosmonaut in the world, Valentina Nikolayeva-Tereshkova, daughter of a simple Yaroslav peasant, started her working career in Yaroslavl. She studied at the technical school and took up parachute jumping in the local aero-club. Daring, tenacity, quick reactions, and excellent physical conditioning brought her, in 1962, into the ranks of Soviet cosmonauts. Honored as Heroine of the Soviet Union, Valentina Nikolayeva-Tereshkova is now the president of the Committee of Soviet Women.

New streets and whole residential districts have arisen in the city based on a general plan of reconstruction. Old houses have been demolished but the monuments of the past are carefully preserved.

Zagorsk, Rostov, and Yaroslavl, together with Vladimir, Souzdal, and several others form the so-called "Golden Ring" of ancient Russian towns connected with each other by highways and railroads. The "Golden Ring" is of special interest to tourists interested in Russian history and the development of architecture and the arts in Russia. In every town and city of the "Ring," hotels for the visitors have been fitted out in ancient buildings, campsites and carparks created, and restaurants built.

Near Yaroslavl the Trans-Siberian Line crosses the great Russian river, the Volga, one of the greatest rivers in the world and the biggest in Europe.

Hundreds of songs have been composed, popular legends handed down, and tales, stories, and novels written about the Volga. It is called "Mother Volga," the mother of the Russian people, the benefactress.[5] Much of the past of the Soviet State, as well as its present, is indissolubly tied up with the Volga.

And perhaps they are right who consider that only he who completes a journey along the Volga from its source to its mouth can understand the soul and character of the Russian. Only then does it become clear where the amazing repose, the firm confidence, the cool patience, and the unyielding stubbornness of the Soviet people originate.

Foreign visitors undertake with great interest trips lasting many days on a comfortable motorship on the Volga, traveling from Kazan to Volgagrad, and further, on a canal westward to Rostov on Don and to the shores of the Sea of Azov.

## Features of the North

The express train has left Yaroslavl. Kilometer posts with three digits flash past the windows. The train is

---

[5] *Kormilitsa:* literally, the nursing mother, or wet nurse.

approaching Kirov, a city on the Viatka River, a tributary of the Kama which flows into the Volga.

Travel-guides classify the climate of the Kirov district as moderately cool. However "moderately cool" is a relative notion; the local weather will be appreciated differently by Russians used to frost and by, say, Italians who love warmth.

"The North, the North, it just smells like it," wrote the great Russian geographer Peter Kropotkin in his diary about these places in the last century, ". . . all that can be seen on the horizon are the pointed tops of the pine trees. . . The neighboring forests are concealed by a grayish-blue mist, the eternal companion of pine forests; from the shore is carried the smell of resin, and the sky itself has become threatening; it is still, becoming chilly." The distance between Yaroslavl and Kirov[6] is approximately 575 kilometers by railroad. The territory abounds in forests, and this has determined the basic direction of its industrial development: the timber industry. From early times, the inhabitants have been engaged in leather, hide, and footwear trades.

Lenin characterized the economic situation in prerevolutionary Viatka in the following manner: "The Viatka and Slobodskoy districts are centers of 'factory-industrial' and 'cottage-industrial' leather and hide production. . . The hide industrialists have hundreds of workers engaged in their homes sewing sheepskins, etc. This constitutes one capitalist factory. . . ."

[6] Originally called Viatka, Kirov was named after S. M. Kirov (1886-1934), a prominent activist of the Communist Party and the Soviet State who was actually born in a small town called Urzhum, not far downstream on the Viatka River.

Kirov is now an important industrial and cultural center with a population of 216,000. Machine building, metal working, and the manufacture of measuring instruments have been developed, and a tire factory, works producing artificial leather and educational-technical equipment, a large power station, and other enterprises have been built. Whole districts of multistory residential buildings, many establishments for children, schools, movies, etc., have been erected.

The city has three schools of higher education, scientific research institutes, three theatres, and dozens of libraries. Kirov is also famous for its accordions and "Viatka" toys. Just past Kirov, we will have completed the first thousand kilometers of our journey on *Russia*.

# Part I
# Photographs

Moscow. Kremlin and Red Square (right), St. Basil's Church (center foreground), Lenin's Mausoleum (above St. Basil's Church). Photograph by V. Yakovlev.

Moscow. Komsomol Square: Yaroslavl
Station (right) and Leningrad Station
(left). Photograph by V. Budanov.

Departure of "Russia" express from
Moscow. Photograph by A.P.N.

Rostov. Church of the Resurrection.
Photograph by U. Sobolev.

"Viatka" toys manufactured in Kirov
(formerly Viatka). Photograph by D.
Herman.

Perm. "Golden Cockerel" Cafe. Photograph by I. Gavrilov.

Ural Mountains, "the spine of Russia."
Photograph by V. Brell.

Southern Urals. Collective farm members family. Photograph by U. Inyakin.

Ural diamonds. Photograph by L. Sher-
stennikov.

Ural Mountains. Obelisk marking border between Europe and Asia. Photograph by A.P.N.

# Part II

# Two Thousand Kilometers from Moscow

## Perm—City of Industrial Boom

The American geographer C. Harris starts his book about the geography of the cities of the Soviet Union with the following phrase: "The U.S.S.R.—the land of big cities." And this is really the case. The vastness of the territory, the immense distances, the difficult conditions of developing the land, and the harsh climate have historically predetermined the suitability of the creation of powerful economic supporting bases—the big cities. It is precisely the big cities which open up the possibility of developing new industries with less expenditure of time and means.

The big cities are the mighty levers in the transformation of nature and the economies of vast and, at times, not easily accessible districts. "Working" for the whole of the country and discharging the function of administrative and economic centers, the big cities draw into the process of active economic life outlying regions whose life had been dominated by centuries old patriarchal conditions and an economy based on nature. This is how the European part of Russia developed.

But such a model of development is particularly characteristic of the Urals, Siberia, and the Far East. There, the cities are comparatively young; the majority of them originated in the twentieth century and some in the thirties, when the Soviet Union set out on the road to industrialization. The Soviet writer Peter Pavlenko remarked: "The principle underlying the birth of cities changed. The military outpost, the fortress, the inn, the transfer point—this is no longer the embryo of the city. The cities grew from factories." This, for example, is the case with Perm, where our train arrives 24 hours after departing from Moscow.

The city grew up near the copper smelting plant which was established toward the end of the eighteenth century. Later, it developed as the center of the metal industry and a port on the Kama River. After the October Revolution, when all the riches of the Urals and all the economy passed into the hands of the workers, the speed of the development of this industrial center amazed even the experts.

All old enterprises were, in effect, rebuilt and began to manufacture new products. A factory producing motors, a bicycle works, mining implement and commercial machine factories, "Kamkabel," a giant factory producing electrical goods, and more than 100 other enterprises were brought into operation. A hydroelectric station with an output of half a million kilowatts was also built.

An even bigger boom started in Perm after oil was found in the region of the Kama River, in the Tartar Republic and near Perm. The biggest oil refinery in the country was built in Perm in the sixties and connected by pipeline with the oil wells. Construction of oil refineries and chemical works was started. Thus, the city of metal workers was changed to a city of oil and chemical workers. It was natural that the industrial growth of Perm brought in its wake a very rapid development of the building industry.

Shoe, clothing, flour, pastry, and tobacco industries sprang up. Today, with a population of almost a million people, Perm is a well-appointed contemporary city. The old inhabitants admire with pride the parks, squares, and tree-lined streets—in the past, seldom seen in the Urals.

Perm is also a major cultural center of the Western Ural region, with a university and agricultural, pedagogical, medical, pharmaceutical, and polytechnical colleges. Theaters and museums open their doors every day, and a number of local newspapers and journals are published in Perm.

The talented young ballerina Nadezhda Pavlova, who has received world acclaim, is a graduate of the Perm Ballet School. At present, Nadya performs on the stage of the Bolshoy Theater in Moscow.

The Tenth Five-Year Plan of Industrial Development of the U.S.S.R. for 1976-1980 provides for Perm the building of new giants: a powerful thermoelectric station and a factory for the production of synthetic rubber.

The industrial rise of Perm continues.

V. Kuranov

# The Urals: The Border Between Europe and Asia

Every school child probably knows of the Urals, a mountain ridge separating Europe from Asia. However, few abroad know that the Urals form one of the largest economic districts of the Soviet Union, encompassing a territory of 824,000 square kilometers. This land with its rows of low mountain ridges and chains stretching from north to south for 2,000 kilometers, has a common history and a common economic development. The western approaches to the Ural ridges are called Preduralye,[7] and the Eastern, Zauralye.[8]

The population of the Urals is represented by several dozen nationalities, the most numerous of which are the Russians, Tartars, Bashkirs, Udmurts, Komi-Permyaks, and Ukrainians. Their settlements are intertwined and present a colorful mosaic. At present, there are about 20 million people in the Ural region.

Close to the Arctic Circle, in that part of the Urals which changes to tundra, there are only a few settlements. Even a herdsman with a herd of deer is rarely encountered. The mountainous part is also almost uninhabited, except for the strips along the railroads where the population density is up to three to four persons per square kilometer. However, along the eastern and western foothills this index reaches several hundred.

The greatest population density is in the Southern Urals where there are many cities, towns, and villages.

---

[7] *Pred*: in front.
[8] *Za*: behind.

Essentially, the land is under cultivation. There are herds of plump, horned cattle and sheep in the pastures. The Bashkirs breed thoroughbred race horses on the horse breeding farms and produce *koumys*, specially prepared mare's milk. There is the belief that koumys has a wonderful quality: plump people lose weight and thin ones gain it. According to medical opinion, koumys stimulates the metabolism, quenches thirst, arouses appetite, and strengthens the nerves.

Perhaps, for an experienced mountaineer, there is nothing to do in the Ural Mountains. But the geologist could find much that is enticing. The Askanskaya ice cave, one of the largest caves of the Karst period, is a rare natural phenomenon: it is a natural ice box. The cave has remained cold since the Quaternary ice period, according to scientists. In the past, the distant ancestors of the Ural inhabitants used to perform their religious rites in this cave. In the South Urals, the so-called "Rescue" cave, according to popular legend, has the miraculous quality of curing people of many complaints. The Kapovaya cave, also in the South Urals, has preserved drawings of people of the late Paleolithic period. Stags, mammoths, lions, wild horses, hairy rhinoceros, and other now extinct animals have been depicted on the walls in color by unknown artists. Representations of some of the animals have been hewn from stone with great skill.

The glory of the Urals as the richest storehouse of useful minerals has resounded throughout Europe and Asia since distant times. Ural iron had already been exported to the West in the eighteenth century. Long ago, copper as well as chrome, nickel, gold, and platinum had been mined here. Every geologist in the world knows of the gold nugget called the "Large Triangle" or "Siutkinskiy," found by the Russian artisan Nikifor Siutkin in the 1840's. It is the largest of the nuggts preserved to the present, weighing almost 35 kilograms.

The Ural people also mine high quality diamonds and emeralds, blood-red rubies, purple amethysts, blue topazes, and golden beryls. The colored Ural stones— malachite, jasper, horn-stone, and marble—adorn the best of Russian and Soviet architecture. In the mineralogical museum at Moscow there are two pictures made of jasper: "Spring in the Forest" and "Stormy Sea, Hot Sunset, and Seagull." The Ural craftsman obviously did not design or assemble these pictures from pieces of stone. He simply cut the stone and polished it. Thus appeared the gray-green foam of the raging sea and the high wave. A fiery strip left by the setting sun pierces the somber black clouds on the horizon. Only the seagull has been inserted, cut from another stone.

Wonderful are the vases and decor of the "malachite" room in the Leningrad Museum, The Hermitage. But perhaps no less beautiful is the artistic casting of ordinary iron. The craftsmen from the town of Kasli have achieved the truly incredible in the "Cast Iron Palace," which is displayed in a museum attached to the local foundry.

Geographers trace the boundary between Europe and Asia along the Ural watershed, but this does not exhaust the part played by the Urals. The boundary is not a fortress wall erected by nature; instead it forms a solid industrial bridge linking the eastern and western districts of the Soviet Union.

Our train rises to the pass across the Ural mountain

range. The mountains have such a gentle slope that the ascent is hardly felt. Only from a distance do the mountains appar large and even inaccessible.

The Ural landscape will be remembered for a long time. Wooded mountain slopes. Bare rocks protruding here and there. Gray-black roads, and a large sun like a copper basin. All this has been congealed as if in thought in the clean, transparent air. There is not even the gentlest wind. Yet it is not hot. The beneficial shadow of the woods and mountains saves the traveler from the summer sun and moderates the air temperature.

Now the train draws to a stone pillar on one side of which is written "Europe" and on the other "Asia." In this moment, there is no passenger who isn't glued to his window. Even the driver, who has passed this place possibly hundreds of times, will not fail to catch a glimpse of the familiar shape. Only in the Urals is it possible to walk with one foot in Europe and the other in Asia!

The Russians established their first settlements in the Urals at the source of the Kama as far back as the eleventh century. They passed on to the local people new work skills and taught them agriculture. In the thirteenth century, the Eastern Urals, the "Yugorskaya Land," became one of the districts of the Russian State. The first industrial enterprise in the Urals, the salt works of the merchants Kalinnikov (on the site of today's city of Solikamsk) operated as far back as 1430. In 1581, the Russian Cossack Fyodr Ermak and his band, on orders of the Czar, undertook an expedition far into the depths of Siberia; a few dozen years later, the incorporation of Siberia into the Russian state was completed.

It was during the same period (in the second half of the sixteenth century) that one of the largest indigenous ethnic groups of the Urals—the Bashkirs—voluntarily united themselves with Russia.

At first, the trade routes from Russia to Siberia ran along the Volga and Kama Rivers and then along the Vyshera and its tributaries. Further on, the barges, loaded with goods, were dragged over land across the Ural Mountains and then along the Tavda and Irtysh Rivers. Subsequently, the settlers found a more convenient route from Solikamsk (on the Kama) across forests and swamps to the River Tura in the Ob basin.

The outstanding Russian historian and geographer V. N. Tatischev worked in the Urals at the beginning of the eighteenth century. He was the first to study and describe the nature, economy, and customs of the population of the Central Urals. Mining of useful minerals, preparation of map surveys, and construction of factories and roads were carried out under his direction. Tatischev chose a new direction for the road from the Urals to Siberia, proposing to build the city which the *Russia* express is now approaching. Called Yekaterinburg in honor of the Empress Catherine, the city was renamed Sverdlovsk after the victory of the Soviets.[9]

For a long time, the Urals have been called the smithy of the Soviet Union. Now they have also become the scientific research laboratory of the country. Many scientific institutions, as well as the Ural Department of the Academy of Sciences of the U.S.S.R., operate in Sverdlovsk.

[9]Sverdlovsk received its name in 1924 in honor of Yakov Swerdlov (1885-1919), an outstanding revolutionary and the first president of the Soviet State.

The famous Russian scientist of the last century, author of the Periodic System of the Elements, Dmitri Mendeleyev, wrote: "The belief in the future of Russia, which was always alive in me, has gained strength and has become firmer from my closer acquaintance with the Urals."

## The Urals Under the Soviets

The transition of power into the hands of the Soviets proceeded in the Urals, as in the whole of Russia, under conditions of a sharp class struggle, but without the bloody clashes that came only after the outbreak of the Civil War. The people of the Urals withstood all the adversities which befell them during that time.

After a period of reconstruction, war again involved the Urals. During the first months of the Second World War, 450 industrial enterprises were evacuated to the Urals from the districts toward which Hitler's armies were advancing. All Ural enterprises were rapidly converted to war production, and the Urals became the main arsenal of the Soviet army.

Today, the stormy development of the Ural economy is accompanied by a profound and manifold study of the nature of the region, of its resources and possibilities as new deposits of coal, iron ore, potassium, bauxite, and rare metal ores are opened up.

## Sverdlovsk—Capital of the Urals

Sverdlovsk, with a population of more than a million people, is the economic "capital" of the Urals.

*V. Kuranov*

A big leap in the development of Sverdlovsk occurred during the last 60 years. Industrial giants were established there: "Uralmash," a factory producing heavy machinery (the equipment for which, incidentally, was made in Perm); "Uralelectrotiazhmash," a factory producing heavy electrical equipment; and "Uralkhimmash," a factory manufacturing chemical equipment; as well as factories producing technical rubber goods, turbine motors, ball bearings, cables, medical goods and many other industrial goods.

Once Sverdlovsk was called "a city without a center." Right from the beginning, it sprawled out so far and with so little restraint that even now there are quite a few sites left within the city boundaries large enough for the boldest architectural projects. The principal street of the city, Lenin Street, is so straight that, standing at one end on the Square of the Communards, one can see as far as Kirov Square on a clear day, a distance of four kilometers.

The plan of the city is in the shape of a gridiron. The administrative departments, educational institutions, theaters, and large stores are located in the central part of Sverdlovsk. The large industrial enterprises are located, in the main, along the banks of the Iset River and near the railroads.

The terrain of the city is slightly hilly. Flat areas of land alternate with small gently sloped depressions and hills. The highest hill is occupied by an observatory.

Sverdlovsk is ringed by pine forests which penetrate the urban fabric in many places. Lake Shartash, the favorite recreation spot of the citizens, is located within a dense wood. Outcroppings of granite in the surroundings of Sverdlovsk resemble picturesque stone tents, as if some giants had set up a camp made of colossal granite slabs. The Iset River has been dammed in several places and forms a chain of small reservoirs.

Sverdlovsk has satellite towns: Aramil, Sysert, Beresovskiy, and others. While our train rolls slowly through these suburbs, may we tell you about an interesting place some 500 kilometers southwest of the city?

## The Bashkir State Sanctuary

We are now in the sanctuary established within the territory of the Bashkir Autonomous Soviet Socialist Republic (capital: Ufa). The sanctuary was established 50 years ago on the recommendation of the famous geologist, naturalist, and member of the Academy of Sciences, A. Fersman. It occupies an area of 50,000 hectares, where broadleafed, mixed pine and larch, and birch forests grow in immediate proximity to the steppes of the Eastern Urals. Valuable exploitable animals and birds (elk, wild goats, martens, squirrels, ermine, capercaillie, grouse) are protected and bred in the sanctuary. Sables, spotted deer, and other rare animals are also acclimatized in it.

The sanctuary has an apiary along the Belaya River where wild bees are kept and studied. This is the only bee farming sanctuary in the Soviet Union. In contrast to "domestic" bees, wild bees easily endure the winter, are resistant to infectious diseases, and are very productive. On the sanctuary's experimental bee farm, some of the bee families produce as much as 200 kilograms of honey during the season.

A visit to the Bashkir State Sanctuary and the apiary leaves an indelible impression. In the sanctuary, the noisy contemporary world, the supersonic speeds, the streams of motor cars are all forgotten, and the traveler is enveloped by repose, by a feeling of oneness with beautiful, untouched nature. The taste of wild honey partaken of at the hollow in the age-old black linden tree is incomparable; honey and air are filled with the indescribable fragrance of the forest and the flowers of the meadow. Koumys and honey, in the opinion of the Bashkirs, is what nature gave man to preserve his health, alertness, and love of life for a long time.

# Western Siberia: The Sensation of a Century

In air travel, time plays remarkable jokes. Recently, test flights of the supersonic liner TU-144 took place between Moscow and Khabarovsk. The time difference between these two cities is seven hours. The plane covered the flight of more than 7,000 kilometers in a little more than three hours. Having left Moscow at, say, nine o'clock in the morning Moscow time, it arrived at Khabarovsk at seven P.M. local time. On the return flight, however, having left Khabarovsk at nine o'clock in the morning, it will arrive in Moscow at five A.M. Moscow time. That means the plane could arrive in Moscow earlier than when it took off!

The time difference between the Urals and Moscow is two hours. After leaving Western Siberia the passengers will again have to put their watches forward by two hours.

The *Russia* express passes the last of the Ural Mountains. The line now proceeds along the West Siberian lowlands which are flat as a table.

This is the largest plain in the interior of any continent on the globe. It has clearly defined boundaries on almost all sides: the Ural Mountains in the west, the Yenisey River in the east, the Kara Sea in the north, and the Sayan Mountains to the south. In its configuration it resembles a huge pentagon with some extended edges in the east and west. From north to south the plain extends for almost 2,500 kilometers, and from west to east for more than 1,600 kilometers. A number of European countries, such as France, could fit into it.

The train crosses Western Siberia for almost two days. In the Barabinskaya Steppe, some 600 kilometers to the east, a majestic picture unfolds before the traveler. The plain extends in all directions as far as the eye can see. Here or there the dark blue ellipses of lakes are visible. The water is completely motionless, level with the low banks or even appearing to be somewhat higher and about to spread in small rivulets over the bright green grass.

In places the steppe is adorned with groves of birches and aspen trees, *kolkas*, as they are called here. From a distance, these *kolkas*, spread out as they are over the boundless plain, appear to merge into a continuous forest. But one could walk for dozens of kilometers without encountering any such forest. Sparse groves of birches alternate with vast spaces overgrown with grass. In these parts, one must have a special sense of direction to find the way from one village to another. It is impossible to memorize any particularly noticeable landmark in the monotonous sameness of this landscape.

Since ancient times the southern part of Western Siberia has been the granary of the country. Millions of hectares of fertile black soil of the steppe and forest-steppe are taken up by high-yield grain cultures; here, too, milk and meat-producing animal breeding and fine wool growing have been developed.

As long ago as half a century, it was thought that the south of Western Siberia should be explored for useful minerals where coal and iron ore were already being mined. However, during the last decades, geologists have discovered major deposits of valuable minerals in the center and north of the district. The most important discovery was Tyumen oil.

## Tyumen and Oil

The West Siberian lowlands near Tyumen are densely overgrown with pine forests. In places the tall pines with their coppery trunks form a solid wall. Only the rare hoots of our express and the clatter of the wheels interrupt the peace of the taiga. A post marked 2,000 kilometers from Moscow flashes past. Tyumen will soon appear behind the trees.

The city of Tyumen lies along the Trans-Siberian Railroad, 326 kilometers east of Sverdlovsk. In the Great Encyclopedia published in Russia by the Prosveschenye[10] Company at the beginning of the twentieth century, this city's population was listed as 29,588 inhabitants and its industry was described thus: "There are 60 factories with

[10] Enlightenment.

1,425 workmen. The largst are the shipbuilding, mechanical, and leather works. There are many small-scale handicrafts establishments, producing Siberian footwear and carpets from raw wool, outstanding for their great durability."

In 1959, there were 150,000 people in Tyumen. Today there are 347,000! Perhaps hundreds of people arrive every day. Some of them stay to work in various shipping depots, stores and factories or join research and scientific expeditions. However, the bulk hurry to the airport with their cases and bundles to continue on their way north. What is the secret of such an influx of new arrivals, unusual even for Siberia?

The principal oil and gas base of the country is being created in Western Siberia, in the northern part of the Tyumen district, in particular. The city has become the organizational and scientific research center for the realization of this large-scale task. On the streets of Tyumen there are people displaying a lively Caucasian temperament—these are oil men from Azerbaijan; and there are the quiet unhurried oil experts from Bashkiriya as well. There are many young people who are starting their working career here, all coming to the assistance of the inhabitants of Tyumen.

The existence of Siberian oil had been predicted by the Soviet academician I. M. Gubkin in 1932, but it was not until March, 1960, that the first well started to spout in the midst of the dense and impassable taiga and swamps near the village of Shaim, at the source of the Konda River.

And then began an advance of people and technology into the area north of Tyumen, perhaps under more pressure and fraught with more difficulties than anything in the history of the world's conquest of nature. People crossed previously impassable swamps into places where no human foot had ever trodden. All equipment, every bolt for these machines, every roll for the breakfast of the oil workers was supplied by helicopter. Taiga midges and mosquitoes in countless clouds unmercifully stung the oil men. They worked covered with special netting, cutting paths through the taiga and erecting drilling equipment.

In the spring, the temporary housing, which, under enormous difficulties, was also delivered by air, was washed away by spring floods. The oil rigs threatened to collapse into the swamps, and the all-purpose vehicles carrying fuel could hardly reach them. Sometimes the oil spilled out of the pipelines and firestorms broke out, necessitating the shipment—also by air—of bulky fire-fighting equipment, including turbojet units emitting inert gas.

Enthusiasm and powerful technology helped the oil men to conquer the harsh nature of the northern districts of Siberia. What has been found and explored north of Tyumen now awaits exploitation.

An aerial bridge links the major Siberian cities with the oil fields. Railroads are also reaching into the swampy region. One of these, Tyumen-Tobolsk-Surgut, has been completed.

Oil already flows through the pipelines. The principal one, 1,000 kilometers long, has linked up with the main Siberian pipeline at Omsk, where it joined the pipelines laid from Bashkiriya to Irkutsk. New towns have grown up in the northern taiga: Gornopravdinsk,

Nefteyugansk, Nishnevartovsk, Uray, Strezhevoy, and Surgut.

In the spring of 1978 Leonid Brezhnev, General Secretary of the Central Committee of the Communist Party and Chairman of the Praesidium of the Supreme Soviet, traveled to the districts of Siberia and the Far East by Trans-Siberian Railroad. The Soviet leader visited 10 Siberian cities, talking to workers, to party activists, and to those engaged in management.

During his stay in Tyumen he met the leaders of the Tyumen district and discussed the implementation of plans for the development of mining and industry in Western Siberia. In particular, Brezhnev stressed the necessity of increasing gas and oil output and of utilizing technology, energy, materials, and manpower more fully and more effectively.

The oil men and the builders must still master new skills and construct the northernmost gas pipeline in the world, from Urengoy and Medvezhyy in the southwest, to the industrial complexes of White Russia, the Baltic States, and Central Russia.

Tyumen has a fine future: industry is expected to double, treble, and grow fourfold in a fantastically brief timespan, and the city will grow at the same rate.

# Part II
# Photographs

Metallurgy plant at Nizhnetagilsk, near
Sverdlovsk. Photograph by A. Lekhmus

Sverdlovsk. Central Square. Photograph by A. Freydberg.

Manufacture of blast furnace bucket ("Uralmash," at Sverdlovsk). Photograph by M. Nachinkin.

"Uralmash" (at Sverdlovsk) production. Photograph by A. Freydberg.

Members of Komsomol Brigade arriving to work at Urengoy. Photograph by M. Nachinkin.

Temporary settlement along construction site of North Siberian Railroad in the Urengoy District. Photograph by M. Nachinkin.

Workers of Komsomol Brigade on construction of North Siberian Railroad. Photograph by M. Nachinkin.

North of Tyumen. Team of construction workers crossing swamp to reach site for erection of oil rig. They were previously dropped by helicopter and continued by "caterpillar" vehicle to the edge of the swamp. Photograph by M. Nachinkin.

New station at Tobolsk. Photograph by
M. Nachinkin.

Drama Theatre at Tobolsk. Photograph by TASS.

Nizhnevartovsk Tyumen Region. Children's playground in residential block. Photograph by A. Lekhmus.

Rig at Urengoyskoye. Tyumen natural gas. Photograph by M. Nachinkin.

Nadia Kharina, correspondent of Nizhnevartovsk Television Studio on gas
pipeline construction site from Agan to
Omsk. Photograph by M. Nachinkin.

Securing of bridge girder across the Agan River, Northwest Siberia. Photograph by M. Nachinkin.

Construction of gas Agan-Omsk pipeline. Photograph by A. Lekhmus.

Tyumen Region. Gas bore hole. Kharasavey Headland. Photograph by A. Lekhmus.

Outpost of gas pipeline workers on the
Yamal Peninsula after one of the fre-
quent snowstorms. Photograph by M.
Nachinkin.

# Part III
# Completed: One-Third of the Journey

## *Oil and People*

Several hundred kilometers north of Tyumen, where oil and gas is produced, lies the Khanty-Mansiy Nationality District. The Khanty and the Mansi speak similar Ugorski[11] languages. Both ethnic groups are hunters and deer herdsmen. Altogether they number 30,000 people.

An interesting incident concerning these people can be recalled:

In 1923, an all-Russian agricultural exposition was about to be opened in Moscow and one literate Khant was required as a guide in the pavilion of the peoples of the North and of Siberia. The People's Commissariat (or Ministry) of Nationalities Affairs requested that such a person be sent from Tobolsk. There was no reply for a long time. Finally it was learned, after getting through to

---

[11] Literally, near the mountains.

Tobolsk over the phone from the capital, that it had not been possible to discover a single literate Khant.

Incidentally, this answer did not surprise anyone at the People's Commissariat. It was the sixth summer since the establishment of Soviet power. The Civil War had just come to an end. Only two years earlier, Vladimir Ilyich Lenin had written in his famous article, "About the Food Tax": "Look at the map of the R.S.F.S.R.[12] . . . north of Tomsk extend vast spaces in which dozens of huge civilized states could find room. And throughout all these spaces there reign patriarchal conditions, half-savagery, and the most real savagery."

Arkadi Loskutov was one of those young Russian people who came to Siberia back in the twenties. He and others left their homeland and traveled to the "end of the world" in order to rescue, under the most difficult of conditions, the former "aliens" from their morass of ignorance, to save them from extinction, and to help them onto the road to a new life. It was an immense job bequeathed by Lenin. It was a feat!

"It took us 10 days by horse to get to Beresov and seven more days along the river to Sosva," remembers Loskutov today. "The little steamship was ancient. You put a small log into the furnace, and the little ship goes slap, slap with its wheels over the water; it is hard to tell whether we are moving or standing still. Finally we reached the place. We built the school but there are no students. The Mansi have hidden their children, they do not want to send them to school, they say that the shaman told them not to. The doctor arrived in the village but no one visits him, although every second

---

[12] Russian Soviet Federated Socialist Republic.

Mansi had trachoma and every third had T.B. . . .
However, somehow, we achieved what we wanted. . . ."

At 20 years of age the Communist Arkadi Loskutov was the first teacher in the small Mansi village of Sosva. He and his colleague Aleksei Goloshubin taught the future science graduate Yevdokiya Rombandeyeva to read the first line of the primer of those days: "We are not slaves. We are not masters."

Decades passed and the Khanty-Mansi District produced its own national intelligentsia and scientific cadres. The name of the Mansi philologist Rombandeyeva is known in many European countries where she took part in scientific symposia.

The indigenous people are becoming skilled in new professions connected with the oil and gas industry. They actively participate in the industrial development of their region as drillers, drivers, pipe layers, and oil rig operators.

Almost 100 oil fields have been opened up in the Khanty-Mansi District, hundreds of kilometers of oil and gas pipelines have been laid, concrete roads constructed, and new towns built. But this is only the beginning.

The second secretary of the District Committee of the Communist Party, L. A. Tailashev, the son of a Khant fisherman, states: "The major national economic complex which is being created in Western Siberia will assure an output of 315 million tons of oil and 155,000 millions of cubic meters of gas by 1980. This was resolved at the Twenty-Fifth Congress of the C.P.S.U. in 1976. It is proposed to lay about 7,000 kilometers of main oil pipelines and almost 14,000 kilometers of gas pipelines during the Five-Year Plan, 1976-1980. Seven hundred forty kilometers of concrete motor roads are to be built and more than 5,000 kilometers of high-voltage electrical power lines installed.

"Oil has a most beneficial influence on the life of the indigenous ethnic groups," Tailashev continues. "You want examples? There is the new boarding school for 192 students in Korliki. Who built it? The oil men. And who built the schools of Okhteurye? And the four houses for teachers next to it? And the boiler house and the pipeline to conduct the heating medium? Also the oil men. At present the builders are starting to erect a House of Culture there and a greenhouse for the boarding school. And who was thanked in Tarkhovo for the high-voltage power line? Again, the oil men. And thus in every small ethnic village, even in the smallest one. Each of these is under the patronage of some oil-drilling organization. The patrons organize visits by concert groups, consulting physicians, and garment workers from community service centers to the small villages of the taiga, bringing them in by air."

There are said to be 12,000 rivers and rivulets in the district, 23,500 lakes, each of an area of more than five hectares, and smaller ones not even considered to be lakes. The helicopter pilots tell how, at the end of August every year, they fly from lake to lake, from hut to hut, and collect the children of the Khanty and Mansi to take them to the boarding schools. The school year starts on the first of September all over the country. Not a single child may be forgotten! However, it is time, dear reader, to continue our journey east.

# Omsk

More than 500 posts with two sets of numbers have

flashed past the train windows since the Urals, indicating how many kilometers the train has traveled from Moscow and how many more are left until Vladivostok. The second day of the journey is about to end. The coaches tap over the railroad bridge across the Irtysh River. The diesel electric locomotive slows down and comes to a halt at the station. Omsk. It has served since long ago as a transport center and a transfer base for goods proceeding north into the interior of Siberia from Kazakhstan and from the Urals.

The great Russian writer Fyodor Dostoyevsky served a term at hard labor in Omsk from 1850 to 1854 for membership in a revolutionary circle. He described the city as nasty and almost without a single tree. Today Omsk has changed into a garden city. Many call it "the greenest city in Siberia," that is how many trees and flowers are there. Light birch groves surround it like a green belt.

In the central part of the city the old Czarist government buildings of the former fortress remain, but new well-equipped houses surround them. More than 1 million people live in Omsk. In the town, there are seven schools of higher education devoted to agriculture, machine construction, medicine, veterinary medicine, road and motor transport, teaching and physical education. Closer to the outskirts are the industrial enterprises and stores.

Today, Omsk is a major center of machine construction, chemical industry, and oil refining. It has advanced into the ranks of the major river ports and railway centers of Siberia. Through Omsk, in the direction of Novosibirsk, passes the railroad with the greatest freight traffic density in the world. Oil tank cars, platform cars with timber, refrigerator cars, and grain cars speed along it interminably, whistling and rumbling. The biggest grain elevator in Siberia is located in Omsk.

The city's citizens maintain that only Omsk deserves the honor of being called the capital of Siberia.

On the street of Peter Nekrassov stands a long two-story brick building, the former "Red Barracks." A large courtyard adjoins the building. This is where the hard labor prison used to be. Within the dirty, smoke-blackened walls of the convict barracks, with its musty air, languished Dostoyevsky. The Czar's court had sentenced the writer and several others to death. The condemned had been blindfolded and tied to posts to be executed by a firing squad, but at the very last moment, the death sentence was commuted to hard labor. Dostoyevsky and the poet Sergei Durov were sent to the hard labor prison.

The great writer, who was put in irons, worked on the bank of the Irtysh River, carried bricks, and fired and ground alabaster. Dostoyevsky described the Omsk jail, the convicts, and their exhausting toil in his book *The House of the Dead*. This was perhaps the only detailed and truthful account of the terrors of the Siberian jails and places of deportation written in the nineteenth century.

The first people in the history of the Russian State to be sent to Siberia were the inhabitants of the ancient town of Uglich on the Volga, for being "negligent" regarding the young Prince Dimitri, who was killed under mysterious circumstances in 1591. Czar Boris Godunov did not limit himself to dealing with the inhabitants of Uglich, who, after the death of the prince, had raised an antifeudal revolt. The church bell of Uglich was also deported to Tobolsk, because its peal had aroused the citizens to revolt. According to the verdict, the "ear" of the bell was chopped off and its clapper torn out.

Deported to Siberia were fugitive peasant serfs intercepted by the police, participants in popular revolts, opponents of the absolute rule of the Czar, and national patriots struggling for the independence of their motherland against Czarist oppression. The deportees played a major progressive role in the history of Siberia. As a rule, they were courageous people with independent views. Among them were many highly educated people: scientists, poets, and musicians. They carried culture into the incipient towns, studied and systematized data on local climate and soil formation, and advanced proposals for economic reform. Former convicts and deportees organized schools, helped in the development of trades, and rendered medical assistance to the population.

Among the most famous "enlighteners" who made a great contribution to the development of Siberia belong the "Decembrists" (the participants in the conspiracy and revolt against the Czar in December, 1825), as well as the writer and philosopher Alexander Radishchev, who published the "Description of the Tobolsk Governorship" and the "Letter About the Chinese Trade"; the writer and philosopher Nikolai Chernyshevskiy, who lived in Vilyuisk from 1872 to 1883; the writer Vladimir Korolenko, and many others.

Vladimir Ilyich Lenin was exiled to the village of Shushenskoye from 1897 to 1900. (We shall describe this episode in Lenin's life later.) Into Siberian exile went outstanding revolutionaries and future leaders of the Soviet State: Yakov Sverdlov, Felix Dzerzhinskiy, Mikhail Frunze, Sergo Ordzhonikidze, Valerian Kuibyshev.

They did not break off their revolutinary activity while in Siberia: they organized circles for the study of Marxism and trained party activists who were, heart and soul, devoted to the revolution.

# Novosibirsk—Partnership
# Between Science and Industry

One-third of the journey to the Pacific Ocean is completed at Novosibirsk.

If the inhabitants of Omsk consider that their city has the right to be called the capital of Siberia, the inhabitants of Novosibirsk similarly have no doubts concerning their own city, that is, if such a capital were ever to exist.

As a matter of fact, Novosibirsk, with a population of 1 million, 300,000 people, is situated even more advantageously than Omsk: at the intersection of important rail arteries to Kuzbas, Kazakhstan and Central Asia, to the Urals and to Western Siberia. Through Novosibirsk flows the Ob River, 5,570 kilometers long, one of the greatest rivers in the world.

Novosibirsk is known as the city of machine builders. The powerful hydroelectric station and all the major plants have been built in Soviet times. There are 40 different branches of industry! The "Sibelectrotiazh-prom" factory, for example, produces different electrical machines for power stations. The power output of the generators annually produced by another factory, "Sib-electrotiazhmash," is approximately equal to the power produced by all the generators manufactured in such an industrially developed country as the German Federal Republic.

The Yefremov works is another giant factory. Metal-working lathes made by these works are as tall as a three-story house and can produce parts weighing a hundred tons and up to 12 meters long.

The Novosibirsk State Theatre of Opera and Ballet enjoys a wide reputation within the country and abroad. The artists of the theatre have displayed their talent in 35 countries of the world.

There are other theatres in the city as well: for drama, for musical comedy, and for puppetry. There are 14 schools of higher education, including the university and conservatorium. Several journals are published in Novosibirsk, including the thick literary monthly *Siberian Lights* and six major newspapers.

Objectively speaking, Novosibirsk has overtaken Omsk in its development.

The history of Novosibirsk began when the Trans-Siberian Line crossed the Ob River. The village of Novonikolayevsk located near the new railway bridge began to grow "as if on yeast." Steamship companies, workshops, small factories, commercial stores, and mills sprouted. Working people streamed from both the West and the East. There was enough work for all.

After the October Revolution, Novonikolayevsk was renamed Novosibirsk. By 1927 its population reached 127,000 people. During the following 50 years it grew by more than 1 million! During the same period, the industrial output of Novosibirsk increased a thousand times!

It is a pity that the train does not stop for long in Novosibirsk. Otherwise one could leave the glass-vaulted station (one of the largest in the Soviet Union), get into a taxi or bus, and make a trip to Akademgorodok,[13] the Siberian Department of the Academy of Sciences.

Akademgorodok, some 20 kilometers from Novosibirsk, was built between 1959 and 1962. It was so cleverly planned and positioned, albeit on a relatively small site, that it gives the impression simultaneously of being both a larger city and a heavily wooded park into which dozens of multistory buildings have been integrated. Squirrels leap from branches of birch trees onto the balconies of the houses.

The academic township is situated along the bank of a wide "sea" which resulted from the construction of the dam of the Novosibirsk hydroelectric station on the Ob River. The broad beach and the waves which come rolling from somewhere beyond the horizon create the complete illusion of a seashore.

In the cozy Akademgorodok live and work many outstanding Siberian scientists. Some 20 scientific research institutes and construction offices, a secondary physics and mathematics school for gifted children, and a series of other institutions are ranged along its wide avenues.

Akademgorodok's scientists helped those engaged in oil exploration to find the Tyumen oil. The Institute of Nuclear Physics created accelerators required by metallurgic and chemical plants. The Institute of Hydrodynamics worked out a way to weld metals by means of an explosion; by this method it is possible to weld together metals which previously could never be joined firmly enough with each other.

---

[13] Literally, academy small town.

The Siberian Institute of Cytology and Genetics is one of two places in the world where the most delicate experiments on brain cells are conducted. The same Institute has taught the animal breeders of Siberia how to breed blue mink, whose fur is highly valued, more quickly and more productively.

In Akademgorodok they not only solve scientific problems, they also teach. They teach ordinary boys and girls. The only unusual thing is that these Siberian children are more gifted in mathematics, and they are taught by academicians and professors side by side with ordinary teachers.

The selection of students for the physics and mathematics school of Akademgorodok is determined by contests in those subjects, organized in all districts of Siberia, even the most remote. The winners are invited to Akademgorodok to take part in the contest's final round. Thus, the truly talented will become students of the school. After 10 years, having obtained their certificate of matriculation, they continue their studies at the local university and then stay on to work in Akademgorodok or prepare to defend a thesis.

One can meet very young scientists here, doctors of science hardly over 20 years of age, and 30-year-old academicians. The founder of the Siberian Department of the Academy of Sciences, academician Mikhail Lavrentiev, formulated the Academy's motto: "Without students there is no scientist."

Guri Marchuk, the present dean of Siberian academicians, says that in the 20 years of its existence, the Department has accumulated a considerable scientific potential and is ready to solve the scientific problems which determine the future of Siberia.

# Part III
# Photographs

Novosibirsk. City Center. Building with
dome is the State Theatre of Opera and
Ballet. Photograph by A. Poliakov.

Ballet: Romeo and Juliet. On the stage of the Novosibirsk State Theatre of Opera and Ballet. Photograph by A. Zubtsov.

"Akademgorodok" ("Academy Township"), near Novosibirsk. Photograph by A. Lekhmus.

"Akademgorodok" Institute of Nuclear
Physics control desk. Photograph by A.
Lobov.

Students at a secondary school, which is attached to Novosibirsk University at "Akademgorodok." Photograph by A. Zubtsov.

# Part IV
# Four Thousand Kilometers

## All About the Taiga

The train continues its course along the Trans-Siberian Line. This is the third day of the journey east. The rail junction Yurga I flashes past the window, and there, approximately 200 kilometers further, is the next stop: Taiga Station.

The novice passenger will look in vain for the impenetrable forest about which he has heard and read more than once. There is no taiga around Taiga Station. It was cleared long ago.

A little further to the east, however, and it will soon appear, this both mysterious and understandable, cruel and kind, frightening and hospitable taiga. And it will accompany the passenger right to the Pacific Ocean, only occasionally giving room to woodless areas.

The great Russian writer Anton Chekhov, who at the beginning of the twentieth century made a journey from Moscow through the whole of Siberia to the Island of Sakhalin, wrote: "The strength and charm of the taiga does not lie in its giant trees and its silence, like that of a tomb, but in that only migratory birds know where it finishes. On the first day one does not take any notice of the taiga; on the second and third day one begins to wonder, but on the fourth and fifth day one experiences a mood as if one would never get out of this green monster."

Chekhov traveled through Siberia by horse, and, for quite understandable reasons, he had somewhat different impressions from those of a contemporary passenger, racing through the taiga at a speed of 80 to 100 kilometers per hour.

In fact, the taiga leaves its imprint on the mind of any person who has been in it even once.

In scientific language, the taiga constitutes vast forests formed by one or several varieties of conifers, sometimes with an admixture of leafy species. Depending on the composition of the forest-forming species and taking into account the density of the forest, the distinction is made between the dark conifer taiga, in which essentially grows the Siberian cedar, and the light conifer taiga in which grow larches and pines. The dark conifer taiga predominates along the Trans-Siberian Line as far as the Yenisey River. The light conifer taiga predominates beyond the Yenisey almost to the shores of the Pacific Ocean.

That is how the encyclopedia describes it. For the Siberian, however, the taiga has many faces. He discerns the low taiga, the swamp taiga, which he calls *sogra*, the mountain taiga which is bright in color and has an elegant undergrowth. There is a Siberian taiga with giant trees standing close to each other. There is a Far Eastern taiga covering extinct volcanos and consisting of frail, black, and sparse trees.

The Siberian taiga comprises seven-tenths of the forest wealth of the Soviet Union. The forests of Eastern Siberia alone represent almost 40,000 million cubic feet of timber.

The pines and cedars do not provide only valuable timber: a cut on the trunk, which does little damage to the tree, enables resin to trickle out and collect in metal containers suspended on the trunk. The resin is a source of turpentine and colophony.

The cedar is a storehouse of tasty and nourishing nuts. These are like sunflower seeds from which oil is gained. The sunflower grows for only one year and has to be planted every year, its fields tilled and manured. But the cedar lives up to 500 years, and bears fruit almost every year. It does not require anything from humans except careful handling when collecting pine cones.

Economically valuable fur-clad animals inhabit the taiga: sables, foxes, martens, squirrels and others. The taiga provides berries: wild raspberries, red currants, cranberries, blueberries. And how many mushrooms! The taiga forest is also the source of wonderful air, rich in oxygen.

Local inhabitants love and appreciate the taiga and its riches. They feel at home in the taiga and while they extract from it much that is needed to man, they know how not to do it any harm.

The development of industry in Siberia has caused an intensive influx of people from the cities and workers' villages of the West, people who have not ever seen an ordinary forest properly. They proceed self-confidently into the depth of the taiga thickets, then stray about for weeks searching for the way out. In such cases, the indigenous inhabitants drop everything and whole villages set out on a search. Helicopters with observers drone above the treetops from morning till night. And it happens often that the lost ones cannot be found.

Hundreds of timber enterprises operate in the taiga, obtaining lumber. The State plan usually foresees not only the extent of exportation out of Siberia of various forest products, but also determines the areas of forest planting on the cleared sites.

Forest fires are the scourge of the taiga. They cannot be watched for from a firetower: the taiga has no end. Thus, dozens of planes and helicopters fly over the taiga in summer in search of likely places of combustion. No smoke, however slight, remains without attention. A team of firefighters is called to the fire by radio and is brought in by air. These are special people, well trained and excellent parachutists; they leap fearlessly from the clouds into the very blaze and fight the fire with the latest techniques.

# Tomsk—City of Students

From the rail junction of Taiga, a short branch line goes off to the north, to Assino, linking the Trans-Siberian Line with Tomsk, a city of 423,000 people.

Tomsk is traditionally considered a city of students. Highly qualified specialists in different fields of science, technology, and medicine graduate from its university and institutes.

There are two theatres in Tomsk, a concert hall and more than 150 libraries, of which the largest is attached to the university; it has more than 2 million volumes.

The city's industry has also grown during the years of Soviet power: new metal, chemical, electrotechnical, and woodworking plants have been built. The match factory, "Siberia," and the metal works, "Metallist," have been reconstructed and extended; a yeast factory, a pencil manufacturing plant, and others have been brought into operation.

Why doesn't the Trans-Siberian Line run through Tomsk? In the historical literature there are quite a few suppositions. Some believe that the municipal administration of Tomsk forbade the designers to let the railroad run through the city (this was, the reader is reminded, at the beginning of the last century) and reinforced its prohibition by a pretty good bribe. Others in the know assert that the Tomsk merchants had offered the designers a sum of money, so that the railroad *would* go through the city, but the builders declined because the site did not permit it. It would seem that the last version corresponds more to the truth. A writer and railroad engineer of that time, Nikolai Garin-Mikhailovskiy, who designed this section of the railway, explained that the rail route to Tomsk was blocked by huge swamplands, and the designers did not want to introduce a "loop"— their main task consisted in laying the rails to Vladivostok.

Those who appreciate architecture will find many ancient buildings, real masterpieces of art, in Tomsk.

Most handsome, for example, is the two-story timber house in which Vyacheslav Shishkov, a writer popular in the Soviet Union, lived. The building is covered with filigree wooden fretwork and resembles a precious casket.

A wide street overhung with the foliage of spreading trees leads to the Lagernyy Gardens, on the banks of the Tomm River. A beautiful view opens from here of the bend of the river and immense wooded spaces beyond. A highway, the Moscow road, winds in the haze, farther on a barely visible village, and, on the other side, almost on the very horizon, is the outline of the cooling towers of the thermoelectric power station.

Not far from the Lagernyy Gardens, scientists discovered a dwelling and graves of ancient inhabitants. There were settlements here even a thousand years before our era. And this is understandable: a hilly dry site, covered with pine and larch forest and close by a big river, abounding with fish.

The so-called Tomsk Tartars, an ethnically distinct group, lived here in the sixteenth century, hunting and fishing. More than once nomads from the steppe invaded the basin of the Tomm and plundered the Tartars. To remove themselves from the danger of invasion, the Tartars petitioned the Czar of Muskovy, begging him to accept them as Russian subjects and build a Russian town at the mouth of the Tomm. The construction of the first fortress on the bank of the river was completed in October, 1604, and this date is considered the founding of Tomsk.

The first university in Siberia was opened in Tomsk in 1888 and later, in 1900, the technological and, in 1902, the Teachers Training Institute. Until recent times

Tomsk maintained the glory and name of the scientific center of Siberia. Now the distinction of being the first is rightfully held by Akademgorodok in Novosibirsk.

## *Eastern Siberia: Mineral Resources of World Significance*

Eastern Siberia comprises an area of 7.2 million square kilometers and constitutes almost one-third of the entire territory of the Soviet Union. The taiga stretches for thousands of kilometers over mountain ranges and table-lands, and there is tundra and permafrost, as well. And yet the thirst for discovery and the spirit to master the problem in hand inexorably drew the Russians into these places. The market city of Mangasea originated in 1600 halfway along the Taz River. The town was fenced by walls built of logs and was guarded by Cossacks. A lively trade in furs took place there.

Seven years later, the Cossacks traveled upstream on the Taz, dragged their boats across to the Turukhan River, and went downstream. On one of the islands, they set up the Turukhansk winter camp, today the city of Turukhansk, then built the Yeniseysk fortress and, in 1628, Krasnoyarsk. Toward the end of the 1640's, the Russians reached the Bering Straits and the coast of the Sea of Okhotsk.

The indigenous population of Eastern Siberia at that time consisted of about 130,000 people, the most numerous of whom were the Yakuts, the Buryats, the Khakass, and the Tuvints. In the main, they engaged in hunting, fishing, and deer breeding, although the Khakass and Tuvints also cultivated small parcels of land, and in the southern part of Siberia even used irrigation.

The appearance of the Russians in Eastern Siberia had nothing to do with colonization of the territory. A major segment of the settlers consisted of peasants escaping from the oppression and arbitrariness of feudal landowners as well as people who were persecuted by the church or the Czarist authorities. In Siberia there was no serfdom. The new arrivals chose any piece of fertile land they liked, plowed it, and sowed it. Since it was not possible to produce a good crop every year, the settlers, like the local inhabitants, turned to the taiga for furs.

Decades passed and officials, taxes, priests, taverns, and shops appeared. And back again was the old servitude.

The relationship between the settlers from Russia and the peoples of Eastern Siberia always remained friendly. And if it happened that the Yakuts and Buryats rose in arms against the debt collectors and the cheating merchants, they never attacked the ordinary settlers.

The complex natural conditions of Siberia brought about the development of the region around separate centers. The passengers of the *Russia* express can see this for themselves east of Lake Baykal and even along the Trans-Siberian Line.

Nature has richly endowed East Siberia with useful minerals. The region is particularly rich in hydro- and thermo-energy resources. Mighty rivers, gathering their water from territories equal in area to Europe, possess immense possibilities for energy generation. The Bratsk hydroelectric power station is already in operation on the

Angara, the Krasnoyarsk station operates on the Yenisey, and the Ust-Ilimsk station on the Angara is nearing completion. The construction of electrical power stations is cheaper here than in European Russia because of advantageous natural conditions: the banks are of rock, and the river bed is solid granite. Thus, the cost of energy output is many times lower.

Coal deposits are also large, and coal can often be mined by the surface, open cut method. Consequently, it is also economical to construct thermoelectric power stations here, which, in fact, is presently being done.

Cheap electric power has made possible in these places the development of industries requiring a large energy supply: production of aluminum, of non-ferrous metals, and of different iron alloys.

All these types of industrial production are not labor intensive, which is particularly important for sparsely populated Eastern Siberia. To be sure, there are no longer just the 130,000 who lived there at the time the Russians came to Siberia. However, while the population has increased several times over, manpower has remained a problem in this austere land.

Eastern Siberia can also pride itself on its iron ore deposits and forest wealth, and it is particularly famed for its gold and diamonds. The region firmly holds first place in the Soviet Union in gold output. The old Bodaybo gold district is as inexhaustible as ever. Gold is mined on the central Yenisey, in the Minusinskaya Basin, and in Yakutiya, where diamonds are also mined. The territory's formerly unconnected centers of industrial development are now gradually changing into contiguous districts and large industrial complexes comprising a series of cities and considerable territories.

Krasnoyarsk and Irkutsk have become industrial centers, while in southern Yakutiya, for example, a whole new industrial district is now being created, based on open cut mining and iron ore deposits. We will tell about this new phenomenon in the development of Siberia later on.

Agriculture has also developed in Eastern Siberia, in spite of the harsh climate. The crops are quick-ripening kinds of spring wheat, barley, and oats. The population engaged in agriculture is essentially Russian.

Agriculture is concentrated in the southern part of the region, close to the Trans-Siberian Line. However, there are also agricultural centers in the north, in Yakutiya, spread over the banks of the Lena River. Wheat can be cultivated even beyond the 60th parallel.

The foundation of agriculture in Eastern Siberia, however, is still cattle breeding, mainly for meat and some combined meat and dairy cattle breeding, as well as fine and medium wool growing. Horse breeding is carried on in Yakutiya (the Yakuts consider that horse meat tastes better than beef), and deer breeding in the tundra zone.

A peculiarity of agriculture is the variety of skills involved. First, there is the fur industry. The territory supplies more than two-thirds of the Soviet Union's output of expensive sable pelts and almost two-thirds of squirrel and ermine. In many villages in which there are agricultural *artels* (collectives), hunting teams are organized. Hunting is conducted in accordance with scientific plans governing the exploitation of fur resources; these plans provide for the reproduction of the fauna of the taiga, as well as for its definite yearly increase in numbers. The collectives often maintain animal breeding farms in which fur animals are bred in cages, especially silver foxes.

There are also many amateur hunters. To travel in the taiga with a rifle is an absorbing occupation, if the person knows the forest or uses a guide. The taiga has an abundance of water and forest game, hares, wild deer, and elk. Here and there, one can hunt bears, muskdeer, and roebucks as well.

Siberia is a wonderful place for those who want to test their abilities in overcoming difficulties, who want to be pioneers for a cause, who want to assert themselves in life. Siberia is a touchstone for determining one's worth and the extent of the will and energy within oneself.

The crossing of the border into Eastern Siberia is imperceptible to the passenger traveling on the Trans-Siberian Line from Moscow. There is the same level ground on either side of this imaginary border: the West Siberian Plain terminates further east. At the end of the third day, we arrive at the city of Achinsk which has a population of 117,000. The city extends along the precipitous bank of the Chulym River and the limitless steppe comes right up to this industrial center.

Achinsk is an important railway junction. From here, a 500-kilometer long railroad runs to Abakan, toward the Kusnetskiy Alatau mountain range. Yet another branch line runs north to Maklakovo. Major milling activities are carried on there. The lumber from Maklakovo is delivered to the Trans-Siberian Railroad, but the logs are floated down the Yenisey to Krasnoyarsk.

The district of Achinsk is a rapidly developing industrial center, characteristic of Siberia. Its pride is an aluminum giant which produces the basic raw materials for the aluminum industry. Thermoelectric power stations based on local brown coal and hydroelectric plants have been built; others are under construction. The Chulym River is being converted into a chain of reservoirs next to which new towns have arisen and are growing. It is assumed that in the future they will form the "Prichulmskoye Ring"—a chain of its own kind of industrial cities adjoining each other and having an overall population of about 1 million people.

## Swiss Alps in Krasnoyarsk

One hundred eighty kilometers past Achinsk lies Krasnoyarsk. Situated on both banks of the Yenisey River, where it is crossed by the Trans-Siberian Line, the city is surrounded by low mountains overgrown with sparse pine woods. If, up to Lake Baykal, the traveler could still see level ground here or there, from the lake right up to Vladivostok he is accompanied by endless rows of small extinct volcanoes, endless like the taiga.

Krasnoyarsk originated on the site of a small wooden fort (*ostrog*) built by Russian Cossacks to assure the safety of the settled Siberian territories against the incursions of nomads. In Russian, "Krasnoyarsk" means "a settlement on a beautiful height, on a steep bank." Yakov Khirpunov, the emissary of the Russian commander, who had selected the site for the future fort, reported to his chief: "This site is on a steep bank, it is pleasant, high and beautiful, the high water will not flood it, there is a forest of all kinds of trees nearby, there are many plowed fields and haymaking fields, and the river is full of fish. One can build the Czar's fort on this spot."

That was in the seventeenth century.

Anton Chekhov, who, toward the end of the nineteenth century, traveled through Krasnoyarsk, found it beautiful and "intelligent," with clean streets, stone houses, and elegant churches.

In 1905, when a wave of revolutionary activity swept over Czarist Russia, the Krasnoyarsk workers, together with the soldiers of the railroad batallion, elected a unified Soviet[14] of Workers' and Soldiers' Deputies as the organ of local revolutionary self-government. At that time, Krasnoyarsk boasted the largest railroad workshops in Siberia, in which more than 3,000 people were engaged.

Having taken power into their hands, the workers and soldiers set up the Krasnoyarsk Republic. The newspaper *Krasnoyarsky Rabochy*[15] started publication.

The Czar ordered the "mutineers" to be subdued by units of the regular army. However, the workers and the batallion which revolted did not take fright. They barricaded themselves in the workshops and defended themselves stubbornly for a week. But the water supply ran dry and the provisions and ammunition were exhausted. The workshops were seized. Trials and executions began. . .

[14] Council.
[15] *Krasnoyarsk Worker.*

*V. Kuranov*

Today, Krasnoyarsk is the third largest city of Siberia (after Novosibirsk and Irkutsk). Approximately 800,000 people live in it. The city has improved its looks over the last several decades and has expanded its boundaries; blocks of new apartment buildings ring the old part of town, which Chekhov liked so much. More than 100 major industrial enterprises have been erected on the outskirts of Krasnoyarsk in Soviet times. Production encompasses harvesters, electric steel, bulldozers, cranes, diesel ships, timber loaders, roofing slate, aluminum, ball mills, synthetic rubber, excavation machinery parts, and much else. Buildings containing a complex of undertakings which use lumber as raw material are located along the right bank of the Yenisey. Here they manufacture paper, cellulose, furniture, cord fabric, artificial rubber, and synthetic fabrics.

The city has more than 700 streets. Thirty-five thousand students and 90,000 school children can be seen on them in the mornings. The Forestry and Lumber Institute of the Siberian Department of the Academy of Sciences and other scientific research bodies operate here. A scientific center is being built near Krasnoyarsk. The Physics Institute, equipped with excellent laboratories and the latest technology, has already taken up quarters there.

The layout of Krasnoyarsk cannot be called successful. In some places industrial enterprises "hang over" residential quarters. The right bank of the river has been developed in a somewhat crowded and disorderly manner. Time will rectify these mistakes, according to the inhabitants. The crowding of buildings in some districts is not particularly upsetting if one considers the picturesque surroundings, where every citizen has a favored spot for relaxation.

Lenin, who lived in Krasnoyarsk for two months on the way to his place of exile, wrote to his mother: ". . . the surroundings of the city, along the Yenisey River, recall either Zhiguli or views of Switzerland: recently I went for a few walks . . . and was very pleased with these. . . "

The famous Russian painter Vassili Surikov (1848-1916), a native of Krasnoyarsk, said: "I have seen the Swiss and Italian Alps, but I never saw such beauty as this, our Siberian [countryside]!"

Several kilometers upstream from Krasnoyarsk, is the Stolby sanctuary. Occupying an area of 17,000 hectares, it includes four mountain districts: Tokmak, Koltatskiy, Esteticheskiy, and Dikiye Stolby.

The sanctuary is crisscrossed by numerous small rivulets and brooks forming deep canyons. The rocks rise high at the watersheds. They are pink-red and, acted upon by water, wind, and sun over the ages, have taken on fantastic forms. Depending on who or what they remind one of, these rocks have their own names: Grandfather, Woman, Granddaughter, Feathers, Sparrows, Chinese Wall, etc.

The favorite recreation area of the citizens of Krasnoyarsk is the Esteticheskiy district. It is also favored by many tourists from other Siberian cities and from abroad. In some places in the forest are the cabins of the *stolbisty*[16]—that is what the amateur rock climbers are called here. The brothers Abalakov, who are famous in

---

[16] *Stolb*: pillar, post, column.

the Soviet Union, started to learn mountaineering in Stolby. Vitali Abalakov writes in his book *The Foundations of Mountaineering:* "Stolby is the spot for games close to the native nest. But after tenacious claws and strong wings have developed, it is time to undertake distant flights to the glory of one's land." On such a "distant flight," Yevgeni Abalakov was the first to climb the highest peak in the Soviet Union—the Pik Kummunisma (7,495 meters) in the Pamir Mountains.

# Lenin's Places

On the evening of March 4, 1897, a passenger train from Moscow arrived in Krasnoyarsk. Vladimir Ulyanov (Lenin), a "political criminal," alighted with the other passengers. The Turukhansk region was to be his place of exile.

Lenin stopped for a time in Krasnoyarsk, to rest after the 10-day train journey. The assistant to the local medical inspector, Vladimir Krutovskiy, managed to get his doctor colleagues to agree on the impossibility of Lenin's living in the Turukhansk region, in view of the condition of his health. Lenin stayed in Krasnoyarsk for 58 days, until his place of exile was changed to the village of Shushenskoye.

On the morning of April 30, 1897, Lenin left on the steamship *St. Nicholas*, traveling upstream along the Yenisey. He went as far as Minusinsk; ice did not permit the steamship to proceed further, and from the wharf Sorokino, Lenin continued on to Shushenskoye by horse-drawn wagon.

Let us, dear reader, leave the train and visit these places.

. . . Our hydrofoil speeds rapidly upstream against the current, southward, closer to the mountains. The village of Ust-Mana comes into view. The River Mana flows into the Yenisey here. Beyond the village are dense forests, places where lumber is prepared for further processing.

The Krasnoyarsk hydroelectric power station, the largest in the world, is located where the rocky banks come closer together, approximately 30 kilometers from the city. It has an output of 6 million kilowatts. The weir of the station raises the water more than 100 meters. A colossal reservoir, 20 kilometers wide and almost 400 kilometers long, extending upstream as far as the city of Abakan, has been formed in front of the weir. In water storage capacity, the reservoir exceeds the Sea of Azov, in the European part of the U.S.S.R.

Our boat has "stepped over" the weir by means of a special ship elevator, and now races along the reservoir. If the vessel were closer to the shore, we could see the famous Biriussinskiye caves. Within the precipitous limestone banks, the caves served as human habitation in remote antiquity. Weapons made of stone, iron, and bone and small implements made of wood and birch bark have been discovered in the caves in the course of excavations.

We are now nearing the wharf at Minusinsk. Along the city's wide, straight streets new buildings are under construction, and the city is immersed in greenery. Minusinsk is a typical agricultural district center. More than 20 enterprises operate here, mostly engaged in food production: meat and flour works, a yeast factory, a brewery, a bakery, and a liquor and vodka distillery.

A lively building program is currently underway in the district. A whole complex of electro-technical factories is being erected using high-speed building methods. Within a decade, Minusinsk will turn into a large industrial center.

A water course branching from the Yenisey skirts Tatarskiy Island, famed for valuable archeological finds from the seventh to the sixth century B.C. In general, there are many ancient relics belonging to various epochs in mankind's history to be found on the right bank of the Minusinsk District.

A large regional museum in Minusinsk was founded by a local chemist, Nikita Martianov, who collected plants, insects, rocks, and artifacts of the indigenous population. In 1877 he opened a modest museum in two rooms of the city school. Today the museum contains hundreds of thousands of exhibits. The library in which Lenin studied is also preserved there.

Within the Minusinsk Valley, the Yenisey forms the eastern border of the Khakass Autonomous Region. The city of Abakan is its center.

An ethnic branch of the Tiurk language group, the Khakass were formerly known as the Minusinsk or Abakan Tartars. Khakass territory has been settled since ancient times. Tumuli and monoliths ("stone women") of tremendous size erected above ancient graves can still be seen even now in steppe districts, witnesses of the distant past. The Khakass once were engaged in hunting, fishing, cattle breeding, and agriculture, in which they used irrigation. They also mined iron ore and obtained iron by smelting. But Ghenghis Khan's hordes devastated the Khakass settlements, and the region lost its independence for a long time. The Khakass became nomadic cattle breeders.

Today, the Khakass Autonomous Region constitutes a national unit with equal rights within the framework of the Russian Soviet Federated Socialist Republic. Soviet scientist Nicolai Nekrassov describes the Khakass-Minusinsk District as it is now: "There are very few districts in our country in which powerful sources of cheap electrical energy combine with such wealth of industrial raw material, and have such good climatic conditions, accessibility to transport, and proximity to the major industrial complexes of Central Siberia."

The Khakass have their own scientists, writers, and artists. The population figure of the region has increased almost eleven-fold during some 60 years of Soviet rule, and today it comprises 67,000 people.

However, it is time for us to leave Minusinsk and to proceed further upstream along the Yenisey.

These days, the village of Shushenskoye, where Vladimir Lenin spent three years in exile, constitutes a sanctuary. The Soviet people carefully preserve the streets, the residences, and everything that is connected with Lenin.

At first the exiled revolutionary, who arrived in Shushenskoye in a wagon, took up lodgings in the home of the wealthy peasant Zyryanov. Lenin occupied a small room: a wooden bed covered with a rough cloth blanket, a small table, four chairs of crude peasant workmanship—that was all. Also books. These remain on small shelves and corner tables.

Lenin worked strenuously in Shushenskoye. In three

years he wrote more than 30 works, among them a major political science work: *The Development of Capitalism in Russia.* So much preparation was required! Lenin read through so much different material before he even got hold of a pen! And all this in the back woods, where mail arrived with difficulty, and where an exiled person had to report daily to the local authorities.

Books were sent to Lenin from afar. As an exile, he was entitled to a subsidy of eight roubles a month. This was spent almost entirely on books. In spite of the remoteness, the hard life, the lack of money, Lenin was alert, never downcast, and he looked with hope toward the future.

At the beginning of May, 1898, Lenin's future wife and companion in the revolutionary struggle, the teacher Nadezhda Krupskaya, arrived in Shushenskoye. She had also been arrested, tried, and condemned to exile. Krupskaya had asked for permission to share her exile with Lenin.

Vladimir Lenin and Nadezhda Krupskaya were married in Shushenskoye. The young couple moved to the more spacious home of the peasant woman Petrova. The house had been built by the exiled Decembrist Alexander Frolov and was different from the other huts of Shushenskoye: above the porch two massive timber columns supported the roof overhang and the windows were positioned high, like those of city houses.

With his wife and mother-in-law, Lenin occupied three rooms. The furnishings were Spartan: a rough country-type sideboard, some cheap crockery, and the invariable table and chairs.

Lenin built himself a wooden arbor below the windows of the house and planted some hops, which covered the simple structure thickly. The exiled family loved to relax in that arbor. In general, Lenin loved manual work. He cut chessmen out of pine bark. He was skilled in making wooden hobby horses for the children of Shushenskoye, and in winter he cleared an area for them for ice skating on the frozen river.

A lawyer by training, Lenin also gave advice on legal matters to the peasants and workers from the nearby mines. He was successful in achieving the reinstatement of a man unlawfully dismissed by the owner of the gold mine.

As a political exile, Lenin had no right to prepare official documents for others—for such transgression, the term of his exile could have been extended. He, therefore, used to dictate the wording of petitions and statements, if one of the peasants asked him for help.

Lenin was also absorbed by hunting. He usually had the company of a local guide, a hunter called Sossipatych in the village. Together, they ranged for dozens of kilometers in search of hares. There were great masses of them in those days in the woods around Shushenskoye, and the hunters usually came back with a rich booty.

The term of exile expired on the 29th of January, 1900, and Lenin's family left Shushenskoye on the same day. They traveled by sleigh over the Yenisey ice. The horses sped past the rocks powdered with snow, past familiar and unfamiliar banks. "We were racing at full speed. . ." Krupskaya remembered later, ". . .and Vladimir Ilych, who traveled without a fur coat, insisted that he felt hot . . . his thought carried him away to Russia where it would be possible to work to one's heart's content."

Eighteen years later, in the Moscow Kremlin, as the head of the Soviet State, Lenin received the commander of the Siberian Rifles, Fyodor Khudiakov. They remembered the Siberian exile, and Vladimir Ilych said: "I fell in love with that land, with my second homeland. . ."

# Where Is the Center of Asia?

Our journey continues upstream along the Yenisey in the Sayan Mountains. The water swirls, breaking against the stony banks and the rapids. Only skilled rivermen know how to steer ships under these conditions.

Before us rises a huge construction site. The Sayano-Sushenskaya hydroelectric power station is being built here. The weir, more than 200 meters high, will dam the Yenisey. The fierce energy of the river will rotate turbines with a power output exceeding 6 million kilowatts. The Five-Year Plan for the Development of the National Economy of the U.S.S.R. (1976-1980) provides for the first units of the station to begin operating. Power will be conducted first to the aluminum works, also under construction in the Sayan Mountains. The station will also supply power to the Minusinsk and Sayan industrial complexes in the near future.

Our motorboat cannot proceed any further along the Yenisey: the current has become even faster, more turbulent and more dangerous. . .

The raging Yenisey appears black between its banks. And then it splits in two. One arm flows from somewhere in the eastern Sayan Mountains, the other from the Sangilen hillside. At the point of confluence lies the city of Kysyl, capital of the Tuva Autonomous Soviet Socialist Republic, which forms part of the Russian Soviet Federated Socialist Republic.

The Tuvints call the Yenisey *Ulug-Khem* (the great river). The site where the two mountain streams meet to form the Yenisey is, at the same time, the geographic center of the whole huge Asian continent. A monument has been erected in the town of Kysyl on the spot which, according to the calculations of geographers, constitutes the center of the continent—a concrete globe rests on a base and a concrete shaft projects toward the sky from the part of the globe representing Asia. The obelisk is inscribed in Russian, in the Tuva language, and in English: *Center of Asia.*

Tuva is an interesting place to the traveler. Its landscapes, which include high mountains and alpine meadows, wide steppes, fast mountain streams, and areas of impassable taiga, are very beautiful. It is said that Tuva is like a magic chest, keeping in store the most diverse precious things: gold, non-ferrous metals, iron, coal, and much else. Hundreds of mountain streams are potential sources of a mighty power supply.

In the past, the Tuvints had no possibility of developing their natural wealth. Speaking different languages and belonging to different ethnic grops (Tiurks, Mongols and others), they were for many years under a foreign yoke. They were first oppressed by the Mongol Khans, then by Manchurian robbers. The Tuvints proclaimed their independence in 1921, and 20 years later requested to the Soviet government to accept Tuva into the framework of the U.S.S.R. The Autonomous Tuva Region appeared on the map of the U.S.S.R. in 1944.

An energetic construction of industries and cities began in the Republic. The nomadic tribes became settled and learned to handle complicated machinery. The "Tuvacobalt" and asbestos works were built. Hospitals, libraries, and clubs began to appear.

In addition, the traditional forms of agricultural production—cultivation of grain, meat and dairy farming, and deer breeding, are also being developed.

Kysyl, the first town of Tuva, was founded in 1914. Today, half the population of the Republic lives in towns. The numerous tribes of former nomads have merged into one people, and a common Tuva language has been created in which papers are published and books are printed. Compulsory universal 10-year education is being introduced, and there are already no illiterates in Tuva, which has its own intelligentsia, its own theatre, and its own pictorial art.

# Two Thousand Kilometers North of Krasnoyarsk

Having returned to Krasnoyarsk, let us make a journey downstream along the Yenisey, on a larg three-deck diesel liner, one of those which circulate on the river over long distances.

The motorship passes the "spit," the place where the Kacha River flows into the Yenisey. The buildings of the aluminum plant stretch out on the right bank, and soon fade out of sight of the moving ship. Other factories show up in turn and dissolve in the slight haze at the back of the motor ship. Krasnoyarsk has been left astern.

The Atamanovskiy "Bull" appears. The steep rocky

headlands on the Yenisey, as well as those on many rivers of Eastern Siberia, are called "bulls."

Back in the last century, a fat lady in a swimming costume was painted on a rock standing in the river. She is called the "Madam," and her color is touched up every year. The captains and pilots determine the water level by the "Madam."

The Yenisey is crowded even though the river is wide. Barges from the opposite direction dominate the traffic. The barges mainly carry Angara timber to Krasnoyarsk.

The Yenisey gradually narrows down. Ahead are the Kasachinskiye Rapids. Although the rocks which projected from the water were blasted away long ago, ships still crowd together near the rapids. The navigable channel is somewhat narrow, and ships can only be let through in turns, a ship moving downstream alternating with one traveling upstream.

We travel north, toward the "white nights." It is difficult to imagine a "white night," which occurs only in high latitudes. In summer, the rays of the sun do not leave the horizon for almost two months. Day is followed by a night which is just as bright. In effect, there is no night. But in winter, night lasts almost two months without a single ray of sunshine. Only now and then, when flashes of polar lights burst into the black sky, is the darkness relieved.

The ship reaches the village of Strelka, where the beautiful Angara flows into the Yenisey. The former is wider at this spot than the Yenisey.

The "empire" of the lumberjacks starts past Strelka. Beautiful building timber grows here, milled by a number of major timber plants.

And here comes the first large city after Krasnoyarsk: Yeniseysk. Once its fame reverberated over all Siberia. In the past century, gold was discovered there, and crowds of prospectors, adventurers, and people with no other hopes for their lives rushed there. The city was bathed in wealth. Then the gold resources dried up. Of the previous glory, there remained only memories and the mansions of the wealth in those days. Yeniseysk had to look for another "specialty." Today it is the city of the river people and an important interchange point on the way from Krasnoyarsk to the polar Yenisey ports of Igarka and Dudinka.

Further down the Yenisey, our motorship crosses the Arctic Circle. Do people live in the land of permafrost? Yes, they do: in small and large villages and even in cities. Along the Northern Yenisey are Russians, Kets, Selkups, and Evenks.

Kets can be found only along the Yenisey and they present a definite ethnic riddle. Their language differs from all other languages in the world, but it is said in their legends, passed on by word of mouth, that they came here in boats from somewhere at the source of the river. As a matter of fact, crockery has been found in the old burial grounds of the Kets, similar to that found in the district of the Minusinkaya Valley, where people were already living 3,000 years ago. Scientists are still trying to solve the riddle of the origin of the Kets.

The Evenks are deer breeders and hunters, and more numerous than the Kets. They have autonomy, occupying the Evenk Nationality District, with its center in the village of Tura.

The Selkups, on the other hand, live mainly in

Western Siberia, most of them in the Tomsk and Tyumen regions. They are descended from the Sayan tribes,
driven north by the Tiurks, and they speak a language
related to the Samoyed group. They, too, are deer
breeders and hunters.

The last major inhabited places on the Yenisey are
the towns of Igarka and Dudinka. Igarka is 1,779 kilometers from Krasnoyarsk. A department of the All-
Union Institute of Experimental Medicine, which inves-
tigates the influence of the Arctic climate and permafrost
on human health operates here. The Igarka Teachers
College of the Peoples of the North prepares teachers for
schools in which education is conducted in the local
languages. The Igarka Musical School for Children
provides a musical education to representatives of ethnic
groups who previously knew no musical instrument,
apart from the shaman drum.

Dudinka is both a riverport and a seaport at the
mouth of the Yenisey. It has a major airport and a
railway station from which trains leave for Norilsk.

Do you realize that here you are beyond the Arctic
Circle, at a latitude of 70° north? This is the latitude
which passes through Greenland and Northern Alaska
in the Western Hemisphere!

# Kansk on the Yenisey and the World Market

We are back in the train on the Trans-Siberian Line as
it drums rhythmically along the rails. It is speeding
toward the sun having already traveled 4,000 kilometers.

V. *Kuranov*

The stations of Yenisey, Tayezhnyy, Kliukvennaya, Zaozernaya, and dozens of smaller ones are past. Soon there will be Kansk-Yeniseyskiy. Of course, there is no Yenisey River here. The city is comparatively close to the Kan River (40 kilometers), but 247 kilometers away from the Yenisey. However, since the name of the new city reminds us again of the great river, let us become acquainted, though somewhat belatedly, with what Anton Chekov wrote about it in 1890: "...I have never seen a river more magnificent than the Yenisey. Let the Volga be a popular, modest, sad beauty, but the Yenisey is a mighty, fierce hero, who does not know what to do with his strength and youth ... I stood there and thought: what full, intelligent, and bold life will enlighten these banks in time!"

While we were reading the travel notes of the writer, the train has passed the Kansk-Yeniseyskiy station. Around the city there is a forest-steppe, a hilly plain with very fertile soil. Wheat, hemp, flax, and maize have been cultivated and vegetables and potatoes grown in the Kansk forest-steppe since long ago. Here, too, are major state farms for sheep breeding and raising meat and dairy products.

The district is rich in useful minerals: brown coal and rock salt. Scientists assume that there are also deposits of potassium salt.

As described by Chekhov, Kansk belonged among the impoverished, stagnant little towns famed only for an abundance of taverns. Soviet power has awakened sleepy Kansk. Machine building and metal working have become established in the city in the 60 years since the October Revolution. A food industry has developed rapidly. And the biggest cotton works of the region have been in production for more than two decades. Kansk fabrics are dispatched to many cities of the Soviet Union as well as exported abroad.

# Part IV
# Photographs

The endless "taiga" along the Trans-Siberian Line. Photograph by V. Chernov.

Taiga in Ussuriysk District in autumn.
Photograph by V. Kasho.

Installation of power line supports on the Siberian electric power system. Photograph by A. Lekhmus.

Spring wheat harvest in Siberia. Photograph by V. Chernov.

Brown bear, a "taiga" dweller. Photograph by B. Korobeynikov.

Krasnoyarsk, one of the central squares. Photograph by E. Ettinger.

In the "Stolby" (columns) State Sanctuary near Krasnoyarsk. Photograph by E. Ettinger.

"Stone Man" in "Stolby" State Sanctuary. Photograph by U. Muravin.

Village of Shushenskoye (Krasnoyarsk
District). Place of exile of V. I. Lenin.
Photograph by V. Shaposhnikov.

Room of V. I. Lenin and N. K. Krupskaya in the house of P. A. Petrova at Shushenskoye. Photograph by V. Shaposhnikov.

Son of a Tuva shepherd. Photograph by
T. Shakhverdiev.

Habitual way of traveling in outlying districts of Siberia. Photograph by E. Briukhanenko.

Village of Aksarka. Mother with children. Nenets ethnic group. Photograph by I. Gavrilov.

Village of Bomak. Amur Region. Evenk schoolgirl on kitchen duty. Photograph by B. Sukhodolsky.

Ice drift on the lower Yenisey at Dudinka. Photograph by Chin-Mo-Tsai.

# Part V
# Half-Way!

## The Baykal-Amur Line—"The Construction Job of the Century"

Tayshet is an important railway junction where the Trans-Siberian Line is crossed by the South Siberian Line from Abakan. Here our train turns toward Irkutsk, to bypass Lake Baykal from the south, while the South Siberian Line proceeds through Tayshet almost due east, to bypass the lake from the north. This is the beginning of the Baykal-Amur Line (B.A.M.),[17] which is now under construction. This new Siberian railroad will connect in the east with the city of Komsomolsk-on-the-Amur. The B.A.M. is often referred to as the "Construction Job of the Century." In his address at a meeting with the B.A.M. builders, Leonid Brezhnev stated that this great construction job was an integral part of a program of great significance to the Soviet State. Today,

[17] Balykalo-Amurskaya-Magistral.

not only has a main traffic line been created, but new villages have arisen and new cities are being established where yesterday the centuries-old peace of the taiga still reigned. The railroad builders are followed by scientists, geologists, planners, and engineers. A little time will pass, Leonid Brezhnev continued, and new industrial complexes will be created in these regions through the labor of man. The B.A.M. will help to utilize the richest mineral resources of Eastern Siberia, and to resolve the development of the Siberian industry in a new way.

Soviet statesmen, rail transport experts, and economists had long ago raised the question of a second rail link with the Pacific Ocean. Look at the map. The distance from Tayshet to the Pacific coast, by-passing Lake Baykal from the north, is much shorter than that along the existing line. Why, then, did the designers at the beginning of the century plan the Trans-Siberian Line so that it by-passed Lake Baykal from the south?

This happened because the natural conditions south of Lake Baykal were more favorable and the population density greater there, and, consequently, the manpower for the construction work more available. The engineers of the past also feared permafrost, and in the south this phenomenon was not universal and could be avoided. Yet even during the construction of the Trans-Siberian Railroad, the experts carried out som investigations into a possible path for the northern line.

In 1930, the Soviet government worked out a general plan for the development of a Siberian national economy. Some broad research into various sites for the future northern railroad was initiated. It was then that the name B.A.M., the Baykal-Amur Line, originated. As a matter of fact, the researchers did not know precisely where in the west the new line would start, from Tulun or from Tayshet, or possibly from a third point. They only assumed that the extreme points would be Lake Baykal and the Amur River.

The construction of the B.A.M. had already been undertaken on some sections prior to the Second World War. Intensive work was proceeding on its extreme eastern section in 1939, from Komsomolsk-on-the-Amur to Sovetskaya Gavan, the port on the coast of the Tatarskiy Straits. It was predicted that construction would be completed in five years. However, the treacherous assault of the Nazi armies upon the Soviet Union interrupted the work.

Railroad construction was resumed when Hitler's armies were defeated at Stalingrad in 1943, and when the outcome of the war had already become clear. Battles still thundered in the west of the Soviet Union, the enemy not yet driven from Soviet soil, but in the Far East more than 90,000 people resumed work on the line. However, the railroad workers had few technical implements— these were needed more urgently at the front.

Night and day, the work went on uninterrupted through frosts reaching −50° and through summer heat reaching 30° Celsius. It is hard to adequately describe the difficulties encountered on the Far Eastern section of the B.A.M. People cut passages through chains of mountains with sledgehammers and pickhammers; they erected bridges standing in icy water; they laid down the railroad bed after felling innumerable trees with ordinary handsaws. Thus were 475 kilometers of the rail line completed.

V. Kuranov

# The Siberian Character

Only the people of Siberia, with a special "Siberian character," could have withstood such hardships. Siberia's own, unusual type of person was formed throughout hundreds of years of struggle with the stern nature of the land. He is distinguished by great endurance; he has a gift for finding his bearings in a difficult situation, and an ability never to fuss and not to become dispirited. The Siberian is somewhat taciturn; he is slow in his movements and in making decisions. He has a distinctive Siberian accent by which everybody can unfailingly recognize him as a Siberian.

Having adopted many of the habits of the local indigenous people, the Siberian has lived with them on friendly terms, and he willingly intermarries. One can discern Asiatic traits in many Russian inhabitants of Siberia. Concepts of national supremacy or racial exclusiveness are foreign to the Siberian.

The Siberian divisions which, in the autumn of 1941, were brought from the East to Moscow played a decisive role in the defeat of the Nazi armies which had advanced to the very walls of the Soviet capital. Sniper units at the front were formed from the Siberians. As accurate sharpshooters, tireless and adept in the art of camouflage, they dealt significant blows to the enemy.

People of other nationalities of the Soviet Union, as well as from the European part of Russia, who visit Siberia involuntarily start to imitate the Siberians and develop respect for them. The word of a Siberian is synonymous with a businesslike and straightforward approach, and with honesty.

Survey work on the western section of the B.A.M. was renewed during the Second World War, and the whole line, from Tayshet to Sovetskaya Gavan, was completed in 1945.

The following story will perhaps help the reader to visualize the conditions under which the survey took place.

In the autumn of 1942 three surveyors,—Alexander Koshurnikov, Dmitri Zhuravlev, and Konstantin Stofato—were working on the first section of the future Abakan-Tayshet line. (Abakan is 650 kilometers southwest of Tayshet.) Koshurnikov, an experienced construction veteran, was in charge of the survey. He had already worked in 1932-1934 on the construction of the line. Using reindeer, his team was finding its way through the taiga with a guide. The latter, however, became apprehensive about the imminence of the winter cold and turned back, taking with him letters written to relatives. The surveyors decided to proceed downstream along the river. They constructed a raft and set off with the current.

Koshurnikov kept a diary during all the time that the team was carrying out the survey. He made the following entry at the Sayanskiye Rapids: "The night was very cold. It is possible that the temperature dropped below 10°. In the morning almost the whole surface of the water was covered with a thin layer of ice. True, the ice is thin and in small pieces, but this is already bad . . . A successive and bad unpleasantness: Kostia Stofato has caught a cold and has pleurisy."

On this day, the surveyors abandoned the old raft, which was soaked through, and began constructing a new one out of dry fir.

This is the entry for the following day: "We completed the raft in the morning and let it down into the water. We took off at 13 hours. We crossed two rapids and, past the second, the river was frozen again for a length of 300 meters. I went to see, came back and decided not to go any further by water . . . we sorted our belongings and took up to 15 kilograms of luggage per person. . ."

They followed the river downstream toward a spot where it was not yet iced over, in the hope of constructing another raft. They understood that they could not get out of the taiga on foot. The distance to inhabited places was too great, and there was not enough strength and food left.

They came to some clear water and constructed yet another raft, but soon it too collided with ice. Again they had to proceed on foot. And again they constructed a raft. And again they had to abandon it.

"It was necessary to abandon the raft. This is alrady our fifth raft. Tomorrow, we shall construct a new one. This is simply ridiculous. Only 52 kilometers are left to human habitation, and these are so insuperable that the possibility is not excluded that we shall not get out at all. We weaken visibly . . . the head spins from even a small effort. Besides, we have been completely soaked for three days. There is no possibility whatever to get dry. As I am writing now, my hand is burnt by the heat of the fire while the page is wet. But the most frightful thing to occur will be when we shall no longer be able to get ourselves some firewood."

On the 3rd of November, 1942, Alexander Koshurnikov made a tragic entry: "I am writing, probably for the last time. I am freezing to death. Yesterday, 11/2, a catastrophe occurred. Kostia and Aliosha perished. The raft was dragged under the ice, and in a moment Kostia went down with it. Aliosha jumped off onto the ice and crawled for 25 meters on water-covered ice. I helped him to reach the shore, but could not drag him out, and thus he froze up, halfway in the water.

"I proceed on foot. It is very difficult. Hungry, wet, without fire and food. Perhaps, I shall freeze to death today. . ."

It was only after a considerable time that his body was found by a hunter.

On the railroad from Abakan to Tayshet there is now a station named "Koshurnikovo" and sidings named "Stofato" and "Zhuravleva," named for the surveyors who perished.

In addition, on the siding "Stofato" there is a memorial tablet: "The construction workers worked here under the direction of V. Stofato." Vladimir Stofato is the son of Konstantin who perished. The son inherited the Siberian character of the father.

# B.A.M.'s Tomorrow

At present only the extreme "wings" of the B.A.M. are in operation: in the west, the Tayshet-Lena-Zvezdnyy, approximately 850 kilometers long; in the east, the Komsomolsk-on-the-Amur-Sovetskaya Gavan.

Workers are being deployed on the other section of the future line, moving toward each other from several points. Tracks for work trains have been constructed over hundreds of kilometers, but since these tracks connect places not as yet shown on the map, there is no point in mentioning these.

Let us depart from Lena Station and follow the future path of the second Trans-Siberian Line. Zvezdnyy, the first settlement of the construction workers, was built close to an old winter shelter used by hunters where the river Niya merges with the Tayura. This is almost the center of the future Upper Lena transport and industrial complex (T.P.K.).[18] It will comprise the Ust-Kut-Kasachinsko-Lenskiy and Kirengskiy districts of the Irkutsk Region, with a population of approximately 91,000 people. The forest has never been cleared here. Consequently, it is most profitable to develop woodworking industries in this area. The construction of three important woodworking plants has been proposed, therefore, at Kirensk, Kasachinskoye and Podymakhino.

Apart from Ust-Kut, there are five other building sites for future stations and villages in the territory of the complex. Workers and machinery have had to be taken to some of these by air.

The North-Baykal T.P.K. is being planned further east, along the northern shore of the magnificent Lake Baykal, and will most likely be oriented toward the tourist industry and relaxation. At present, the population of the complex consists of some 19,000 deer breeders, fishermen, and hunters.

The Mokskaya hydroelectric power station (proposed output: 1.5 million kilowatts) is to be built on the Vitim River which has an abundance of rocky narrows.

[18] T.P.K.: *Transportno-Promyshlennyy Komplex.*

The station will supply power to the adjoining section of the B.A.M.

The South Yakutiya T.P.K., which includes the Aldan gold mines, rich iron ore deposits, and a recently discovered coal basin, is being built further east. The coal reserves here are estimated at some 40,000 million tons. Japan is participating in the Yakutiya basin project on a compensation basis: represented by the Minam Jakutotan Kaihazu Kiorioku Company, Japan is delivering, on credit, machinery and equipment worth 450 million dollars and will receive coking coal in exchange.

The open cut mine on the coast of the Neryungri River (with an output of 12 million tons a year) will be the first to be exploited. An enrichment plant producing 9 million tons of concentrate will also begin operations here. Coal has been mined in these places since 1966. At present, it serves the needs of the B.A.M.

Amidst mountains and snow, open cut mines of copper ore of Udokansk origin is scheduled to begin. The enriched concentrate will be shipped by the B.A.M. to the East Siberian copper-chemical plant planned at Nerchinsk.

More than 100 kilometers of rail have already been laid in the district of the South Yakutiya T.P.K. Further east is the West Amur T.P.K. The present workers' settlement Tynda, or Tyndinskiy as it is officially called, will become its principal city. The territory is distinguished by fierce frosts, swampy moors, and a plethora of rivers which freeze right to the bottom in the winter. Only 32,000 people live in this district at present, mainly hunters and deer breeders who lead a nomadic life with their herds.

In the district, there is gold, silver, and other useful minerals, but large industry is not intended for Tynda; the city will be a base for the interchange of goods proceeding to places of production based on natural resources. Tynda, then, is to become an important transport center.

Further east again will be the Zeysko-Svobodenskiy T.P.K. Its development will be based on the hydroelectric power station (projected output: 1.28 million kilowatts) to be erected on the Zeya River, and on the exploitation of the forest wealth of the region. A major timber industry center is proposed at Zeysk.

Still further east in the B.A.M. district will be the Urgalskiy T.P.K. (based on coal mining and the timber industry) and the Selemdzhinskiy T.P.K. (forest exploitation).

The Lower Amur T.P.K. will comprise such industrial cities as Komsomolsk, Nikolajevsk, and Amursk. The basis of a building industry is already being created along the whole course of the B.A.M.; woodworking plants, factories for prefabricated components of residential buildings, and plants manufacturing steel constructions. Major quarries for aggregate, gravel, and other building material have come into operation.

Not only is a second railroad being built, but a solid foundation is being laid for the industrial future of the whole of Siberia.

## The Manpower Problem

It is quite obvious that the B.A.M. line will run through a sparsely populated area. In these parts, which are difficult to live in, a human being is less frequently encountered than, say, a fur-clad animal. There has always been a lack of manpower in Siberia and the Far East. Now, the laying of 3,200 kilometers of tracks on that line is planned, as well as several large cities with a population of up to 200,000 and 56 settlements in which 30,000 railroad workers alone will live. In addition, manpower is required for forest industries and coal mining, for work in new mines, and for the erection of new power stations.

Where will the manpower for the B.A.M. come from? Before the Second World War, the shortage in manpower in Siberia and the Far East was made up by settlers from European Russia. However, the problem has become complicated by the development of industry literally in all corners of the Soviet Union, including its central parts. Siberia and the Far East have already taken their share: during the last 15 years, 150 new cities and villages have arisen there.

The planners see two ways of overcoming the problem. The first is by the influx, although at a lesser rate than in the past, of workers, especially young people, from already developed places. Young people are more mobile, less demanding with regard to life's comforts, which, as a rule, are lacking in the first stage of an area's development. They are driven by the romantic notion of pioneering. They are offered higher incomes and facilities to acquire a higher or specialized education at their place of work.

The second solution to the manpower problem is to attract the local population to work in construction and industrial enterprises. Today, the youth of the local nationalities have a good general educational background and tend to relinquish the occupations of their fathers and grandfathers and settle in the cities. Local young people should be a reliable source of labor reserves for the B.A.M. and for Siberia as a whole.

However, one must not think that all questions of labor in this biggest construction job of our century are resolved easily and simply. In order for the new arrivals to become permanently established on the B.A.M., their conditions of work and their earnings must match those of places already developed. But residential construction is several times more expensive in Siberia and the Far East. To move one person on the B.A.M. into a well-appointed dwelling provided with residential amenities requires, according to economists' estimates, approximately 25,000 roubles (1 rouble = $1.38).

It is also necessary to do battle with the scourge of Siberia and the Far East, bloodsucking insects called *gnous*. Oldtimers like to tell a nightmarish story to the novices: a man, they say, went through the taiga, encountered a wolf and, in his fright, climbed a tree but fell off. However, he did not really fall, for millions of mosquitoes caught him.

This, of course, is an exaggeration. But the gnous and mosquitoes are really a serious problem, causing discomfort and spreading disease. Special protective nets and special clothing are necessary, even though the latter impedes movement.

Special scientific research institutes are working to design new types of protective clothing and improved insect repellents. Special machines spread chemical compounds over large areas. The "gnous" will be defeated, of course, since the state does not stint on funds and efforts in this respect.

The scientific development of natural resources and of energy, and transport, the battle against the insects, the need for manpower and decent housing, the financing of the work—all these problems must be resolved simultaneously, according to a clearly worked out long-range plan. This is why the real possibilities of a much wider development of Siberia and the Far East have appeared only now.

## Nizhneudinsk: Waterfall and Caves

Buildings under construction at Tayshet, where the B.A.M. starts, move slowly past the windows, and the *Russia* picks up speed and rushes further east to Nizhneudinsk.

In the distant past, this city was an interchange and trading point between the indigenous people and the Russian pioneers in Siberia. Later, merchants began to ship their goods to bigger cities, and Nizhneudinsk became a quiet town without administrative function. Even the great Siberian Line did not disturb the provincial, unhurried rhythm of its life.

Only in 1932 did the first industry, a mica factory, appear in Nizhneudinsk. In the last decade, however, the city seems to have made up for lost time by becoming an industrial and logging center with a railroad station that sees a large turnover of goods. The Uda River, which flows through the city, looks well in its surroundings of residential and industrial buildings.

Some 18 kilometers from the city is one of the most beautiful places in Siberia, the Ukovskiy Waterfall.

Formed as the Uda River tumbles from a height of 20 meters into a narrow gorge, it is relatively small but very picturesque, framed as it is by taiga trees. The water runs along natural stairs of wild rock, and it all seems like the work of a skilled architect and artist.

Seventy-five kilometers upstream along the Uda is a mountainous district with another famous natural spot, the Nizhneudinskiye caves. These are located 450 meters above the river and are often visited by local inhabitants, as well as by historians and geographers.

In the country up the river, where other Siberian rivers, the Biryusa and Iya, have their source, live the Tofalars, or Tofy. Administratively, the territory forms part of the Nizhneudinsk district. There are only 600 to 700 Tofalars. They are cut off from the rest of the world by mountain ridges and gorges and can be reached only by helicopter.

The Tofalars belong to one of the ethnic branches of the Tuvints. In ancient times, they led a nomadic type of life. Today, the Tofalars have several permanent settlements and have learned to till the land. They combine agriculture with deer breeding and hunting.

The study of the life, folklore, and customs of the Tofalars helps scientists in their research into the history of the indigenous population of the Sayan Mountains.

Continuing east along the Trans-Siberian Line, we come to Tulun, another woodworking center. It has saw mills, woodworking plants, and hydrolysis works. Coal is mined on the outskirts of the city, and quartz sand is also obtained here. Glass manufacture based on this raw material originated in Tulun itself.

Agriculture has been developing in the Tulun-

Irkutsk forest-steppe since early days. The first Cossacks had remarked that in these parts there were "suitable lands for plowing and grazing and haymaking, and fishing was very close."

In Soviet times, animal husbandry was introduced into local villages or directly on pastures, and mills, grain elevators and butter factories were built on the settlements near the railroad stations. Experimental agricultural stations were established at Tulun and Irkutsk. In 1941, Predbaykalye[19] was already producing three times as much grain as in 1913, and the output from the animal breeding rose sharply.

Our train has already passed Tulun, from which a highway goes on to Bratsk, a new industrial city. Should we not visit there?

# Bratsk: A New City in the Taiga, a New Industrial Complex

We are off to Bratsk. There are taiga thickets on both sides of the highway and intensive traffic on the road. Many of the trucks carry building materials and machinery for the hydroelectric station under construction at Ust-Ilimsk. Others, traveling in the opposite direction, transport wood for the Tulun enterprises and iron ore from the Ilimsk mines.

Ahead lies Bratsk—a modern city which grew up during the last 20 years in the midst of wild, uninhabited places. Around Bratsk are some rather busy villages

[19] Land in front of Lake Baykal.

several kilometers apart: Ossinovka, Porozhskiy, Tshek-anovskiy, Energetic, and Padun.

The center of Bratsk, with rows of multistory buildings, slopes to the bank of the reservoir. The whole coastal strip is planted with young gardens.

The highway runs up to the Angara River and to the weir of the Bratsk hydroelectric station, about 10 kilometers from the city. Once this was the site of the Padunskiye Rapids; now there is the weir and a deep sea. Lumber floated down the river is unloaded and prepared for processing in the bay some 20 kilometers from here. Up to 6 million cubic meters of lumber are processed; in addition, 200,000 tons of cord cellulose, 280,000 tons of cardboard, 250,000 cubic meters of plywood, and 450,000 tons of paper are produced yearly in the Bratsk timber complex, which is famous all over the Soviet Union. The plans for the national economy provide that the forests cut down along the banks of the Angara will gradually be restored.

The water storage reservoir of the Bratsk hydroelectric station, named in honor of the 50th anniversary of the October Revolution, is the largst artificial lake in the world, with a maximum depth of 160 meters. It extends for 570 kilometers and has considerably improved navigation on several rivers, the Angara, Iya, Uda, Ossa, and others. The colossal quantities of water, conserving heat for a long time have considerably softened the climate on the shores of the Angara River. The winters are now 5 to 7° warmer here than deep in the taiga.

Two powerful hydroelectric stations will operate further downstream on the Angara. Surveys are being conducted at the site of the proposed Boguchanskaya

H.E.S., and the Ust-Ilimsk H.E.S. (producing 4.5 million kilowatts) is nearing completion. A large modern city has already grown up near the Ust-Ilimsk power plant.

Today, 53,000 people live in Ust-Ilimsk and its population is growing daily. A branch line from the B.A.M. station Khrebtovaya has been extended to the city. A huge forest industry complex is being built nearby, with the participation of several socialist states.

Close to Ust-Ilimsk lies Zheleznogorsk, which was declared a city on September 20, 1965. It has spread out in the shape of a typical amphitheater on the slopes of the Zheleznaya Mountain, facing the Korshunikha River and the Tayshet-Lena Railroad. Nine-story apartment houses climb higher and higher up the mountains overgrown with trees.

On the other bank of the river are the buildings of the mineral enrichment plant, working over 15 million tons of iron ore per year.

## *Predbaykalye—"The Siberian Salt Cellar"*

The train speeds southeast toward Irkutsk, across the territory of the Ust-Orda Buryat Nationality District.

The Ust-Orda Buryats differ in language and customs from the so-called East Buryats, who live in the Buryat Autonomous Soviet Socialist Republic (which the train will reach in half a day).

The Buryats, who were nomads, began a settled way of life under the influence of Russian settlers. After the October Revolution, life in the district underwent a transformation. Today, more than 150,000 people live here. Where the Buryats had once been an illiterate people, they now have four newspapers of their own, books, radio, and television. More than 100 libraries and 300 cultural centers and clubs have been built for them. Among the Buryats now are more than 100 major scientists, as well as their own writers, artists, and generals.

Only colorful festivals have remained from the Buryats' previous nomadic life. The most interesting of these is the harvst festival—Surkharban. All the adults gather for it. Traditional horse races are held, as well as competitions in archery and a national form of wrestling. It is interesting to note that among the best Soviet wrestlers are many Buryats, people who have imbibed the skill and will for victory with their mother's milk.

The train passes a town with the poetic name of Zima.[20] The next important inhabited center is Cheremkhovo.

In its time, the village of Mikhailovskoye stood here. Beneath it were coal deposits, but the inhabitants were not interested in coal. They continued to use firewood for heating, according to Russian custom. After the Trans-Siberian Railroad was constructed, coal was needed for the locomotives. Thus, one mine after another was opened in this district.

During the First World War, the male population of the mining villages was drafted into the army, and the mining of coal in Cheremkhovo ceased. The mines collapsed and the mining equipment deteriorated.

The miners who returned home after the final

[20] Winter.

victory of the Soviets in Predbaykalye wrote a letter to Lenin, promising to resume coal production in the shortest possible time and overcome the postwar collapse. The workers of Cheremkhovo kept their word. Coal production was rapidly restored.

In the thirties new mines were established, but since 1949, coal at Cheremkhovo has been obtained by the open cut method. Twenty million tons of coal are mined here every year.

The city has grown to a population of nearly 87,000 people for whom the usual facilities—schools, theatre, libraries, and workers' clubs—are provided.

Not far from the city, in the village of Belsk, stands a watchtower blackened by time. This is all that remains of a wooden fortress constructed here in 1691 by Russian Cossacks as a defense against warlike nomadic tribes.

Next on the railroad to Lake Baykal is Usolye-Sibirskoye, called the "chief Siberian salt cellar." It is a city of more than 100,000 inhabitants.

Rock salt deposits in the district are estimated at the truly astronomic figure of more than 20 billion tons. Obtained in huge quantities, the rock salt is processed in the salt works, shipped to many cities within the country, and exported abroad.

The factories in Usolye-Sibirskoye produce plywood and matches and process leather. If "Baykal" is found inscribed on a match box label, it means that the matches were made in this city.

Near the salt mines is the health resort "Usolye." About 5,000 people with afflictions of the limbs or suffering the after-effects of poliomyelitis come here every year. The basic therapeutic remedies of the resort are mineral waters containing salt and sulfur, and mud baths.

Not far from Usolye-Sibirskoye are the villages of Malta ("black alder place" in Buryat language) and Buret, where the Soviet archeologists M. M. Gerassimov and A. P. Okladnikov, in 1928 and 1936, discovered the Maltinskoye settlement and an abode going back to the stone age. The archeologists found the remains of ancient dwellings, different implements made of stone, small bone statues, representations of women and birds, small flint weapons, and artistic adornments made from the tusk of a mammoth.

There is one more historical place not far from the city—the village of Alexandrovskoye. In it, the hard labor prison "Alexandrovskiy Zentral," was built at the end of the nineteenth century. Reports of its harsh conditions spread terror throughout the whole of Czarist Russia. This was where the participants in the 1905 revolution were held. Popular legends and songs have been composed about the Alexandrovskiy Zentral, and it was often mentioned in the memoirs of old revolutionaries.

A little beyond Usolye-Sibirskoye, the train passes the small station of Polovina[21] and the conductor never fails to inform the passengers that the express has traveled halfway from Moscow to Vladivostok. This has already become a tradition. Let us be truthful, however, and reveal to the reader a "great secret": from Polovina to Moscow it is 5,090 kilometers and to Vladivostok 4,212 kilometers! The point of the line at which the distances from the capital and the Pacific Ocean are

[21] Half.

equal is, in reality, west of Nizhneudinsk.

Actually, Polovina was at one time in the center of the great Trans-Siberian Railroad, but that was when the line did not run through Sverdlovsk but through Chelyabinsk, and not along the bank of the Amur but through Manchuria.

# Part V
# Photographs

Young people arriving at Tynda to take part in construction of Baykal-Amur Railroad. Photograph by A. Lekhmus.

Construction of Baykal-Amur Railroad.
Photograph by M. Nachinkin.

Residential districts of Tynda. Photograph by A. Lekhmus.

Timber industry complex at Bratsk.
Photograph by P. Malinovsky.

Workers of timber industry complex at Bratsk on day off. Photograph by M. Nachinkin.

Bridge over the Angara near Bratsk.
Photograph by E. Briukhanenko.

Bratsk hydroelectric power station.
Photograph by N. Malinovsky.

# Part VI

# The Post Marks Six Thousand Kilometers

## Angarsk

Angarsk is a young city. It was founded in 1946 on the right bank of the Kitoy River, near where the Kitoy flows into the Angara. There were no extensive areas subjected to permafrost here. The builders were charmed by the level valley, the young pine forest, and the wonderful air.

Within 30 years the population of the city reached almost a quarter of a million. The reason for such rapid growth does not lie in a high birth rate, although such is actually the case since mainly young people live here, but in the unending stream of new settlers who work in chemical, oil-refining, and power plants and in light industry. Angarsk has not only caught up with the Siberian cities which were more advanced in industrial production, but has overtaken them.

V. Kuranov

Science contributed greatly to this. The research institutes and a whole range of scientific establishments at Angarsk conduct continuous research in many of the exact sciences and in the humanities. Of particular significance is the part played by the chemical research institutions: the Department of the Scientific Research Institute of Chemical Machine Construction and the Institute of Oil and Coal Chemistry Synthesis.

Angarsk is the best appointed city of East Siberia. Apartment blocks of concrete and glass alternate with sports structures, swimming pools, and areas for walks and recreation. The city is set off by high-rise buildings.

In popular legends, the Angara River is called the only daughter of Lake Baykal. Many rivers flow into the lake, but only the Angara flows out of it. This Siberian beauty is fast, its water always high, clean, and cool. It is distinguished among other Siberian rivers by a singular phenomenon: it does not freeze for many kilometers, even during the most severe frosts. Only below Irkutsk, sometime in the middle of January, does the river become covered with ice. The steam which rises above the river during heavy frost adorns the trees and shrubs with hoar frost, as it does the houses along the banks as well. Siberian people call the silver lace of the Angara hoar frost *kurzhak*.[22] On certain days the mist above the river becomes so dense that cars must put on their headlights and travel at minimum speed.

The length of the Angara is not very great—about 1,800 kilometers. The river is navigable only from Irkutsk to the weir of the Bratsk power station. Beyond the weir, the Angara is cut by rapids in many places, becoming navigable again after being joined by the tributary Ilim.

[22] Related to *kruzhevo*: lace.

The basic distinguishing quality of the Angara is its immense energy potential. According to the estimates of experts, it is possible to erect on the Angara a whole cascade of electric power stations with a total output of 18 million kilowatts.

# Irkutsk: Furs for International Auction

In the year 1661 Ivan Pokhabov, the commander of a Cossack detachment, wrote to the governor of East Siberia in the city of Yeniseysk: "Salutations to Ivan Ivanovich (governor by the grace of the sovereign Czar, Grand Duke Alexei Mikhailovich, and autocrat of the whole of Great, Little, and White Russia), from the Yenisey nobleman's son, Yakunka Ivanov Pokhabov. In this 169th (1661) year, on the 6th of July, I am erecting with servicemen the sovereign's new stockade on the Verkholenskaya side; the towers and the ceiling are erected and the sovereign's corn barn is in the course of construction by the servicemen, and there is a tower on the barn. . ."

The Irkutsk stockade soon contained more than 40 houses, and both peasants and tradesmen settled in it, in addition to the Cossacks.

The rapid rise of Irkutsk as a trading center was facilitated by a convenient location at the intersection of the great historic road crossing Asia to the Pacific Ocean and the Angara waterway connecting Lake Baykal with the Yenisey. In time, more substantial log walls and towers grew up around that intersection. In 1682, the stockade became the center of the independent Irkutsk province.

The Buryats and Evenks, who had lived on the shores of Lake Baykal since ancient times, were accepted into the service of the Irkutsk fortress and replenished the Cossack detachments. They became tradesmen and even rose to higher office. For example, documents dating back to 1693 tell about the elevation of a man named Taishik to the position of "a boyar's son" (an aristocrat). His name was then changed to Peter Ivanov.

In 1714, Irkutsk was visited by Chinese envoys on their way to Khan Ayuk. In a translation of that time from the Chinese into the Russian language, Irkutsk is described in detail.

"There are more than 800 families in it, and these live in timber homesteads constructed of logs with towers and attics which are built, however, more in the Russian than the Mongol manner. . .

"One finds in the possession of the inhabitants: beds, tables, ordinary armchairs, benches, carriages, carts, large and small sleighs and boats. Among musical instruments they have: bells, drums, wooden flutes, and dulcimers and violins with copper strings. They manufacture white linen cloth from flax and Russian leather from cow hides.

"Among cereals there grow: rye, wheat, buckwheat, oats, barley and hemp; in the orchards: radishes, carrots, turnips, cabbages, onions and garlic. Of domestic animals there are: horses, cows, sheep, pigs, also fowl, ducks, dogs and cats. The inhabitants are generally content with water from wells, and say that in the Angara there are all kinds of fish."

In July, 1890, Anton Chekhov made the following note about Irkutsk in his notebook: "Of all Siberian cities, the best is Irkutsk . . . Irkutsk is an excellent city. Quite intelligent. A theatre, a museum, a city park with music, good hotels. . . . There are no ugly fences, absurd signboards and vacant lots with inscriptions stating that it is not allowed to stop."

The first train arrived in Irkutsk on August 29, 1898. The water works were constructed in 1905, and a year later a small local power station started to supply electricity.

Irkutsk used to be resplendent with the mansions of the wealthy. There was an institute for noble ladies and secondary schools for the children of the urban notables. Here and there, on the outskirts, were the wretched huts of the poor.

Today, Irkutsk is a major industrial center of East Siberia, with more than 70 big factories. Production includes dredges for the gold and diamond mining industries, blast furnace equipment, lathes, and casting machines for metallurgy. Goods made in Irkutsk are exported to India, Vietnam, and other Asian countries.

Irkutsk is also the largest center of the fur trade. Sable, ermine, squirrel, mink, and other salable furs are taken to the famous Leningrad fur auction, where business people from many lands gather annually.

Thanks to its geographic position, Irkutsk has long been the home of different administrative institutions. Today the following are established there: the East Siberian Planning Commission, the East Siberian Administration of the Civilian Aerial Fleet (Aeroflot), the Administration of the East Siberian Railroad (which is a part of the Trans-Siberian Line), different kinds of building and installation organizations, and institutions of higher education.

Irkutsk is a clean, cozy city with a population of 523,000. On the Angara embankment there is a park and a monument to the outstanding explorers of Siberia. It is always lively there. In summer, people drive out to the picturesque bays of the reservoir, formed after the construction of the Irkutsk hydroelectric station on the Angara.

During the last decade, Irkutsk has been visited by tens of thousands of foreign tourists: the city itself and its history are interesting and a journey to Lake Baykal (along the Angara or by car) is a memorable experience.

Many undertake excursions from Irkutsk to Bratsk.

# Lena Gold

A passenger on the Trans-Siberian train cannot see the Lena River. Its source is north of Irkutsk in the Baykal mountain range. However, one cannot travel through the whole of Siberia and not know about the Lena gold fields. Let us mentally transfer ourselves to the city of Bodaybo, which stands on the high bank of the Vitim, a tributary of the Lena.

The first gold field was officially registered here on September 19, 1848. The news of the Siberian riches spread rapidly throughout the whole world. "Gold fever" raged along the Vitim and the Lena. Some companies obtained 200 to 600 *poods*,[23] and sometimes as much as

[23] A weight of 40 Russian pounds=16 kilograms.

1,000, per year. It was here that the British concession "Lena Goldfields" was established.

The Russian writer Ivan Goncharov (1812-1891), who spent some time in these places, described what he saw: "Last night I passed the so-called 'cheeks,' one of the sights of the Lena. These are immense, majestic cliffs, such that I had rarely seen at the seashore. If you drive near the base, the carriages and their horses look like crawling insects. These rocks are terribly carved up, wild and frightening, so that one would like to pass them quickly."

Add to this extreme frosts in winter, exhausting heat in summer, and an absence of roads, and a picture emerges of the Lena gold fields of those days, when enterprising prospectors appeared there.

Labor was poorly paid, the conditions of life were almost like those of hard labor, the mines' administration exercised power arbitrarily, and lawlessness went "unnoticed" by the authorities.

And yet, over a period of 80 years, this district yielded up fantastic riches to the owners, 40,000 *poods* of pure gold!

The events of 1912 have already been mentioned: the shooting down by Czarist executioners of workers engaged in a peaceful demonstration. Every year people from all corners of the land come to the monuments erected on the spot where the demonstrators were fired on, and to the cemetery to place flowers in honor of those who perished.

Today, a regular connection by air has been established between Bodaybo and Irkutsk. Everything in Bodaybo has undergone a transformation. Powerful floating dredges, excavating machinery, and conveyors have replaced the primitive implements of the prospectors. There are well-appointed dwellings, polyclinics, workers' clubs, libraries, and movies in the city and in the villages of Mamakan, Artyemovsk, and Drazhnyy. A bread factory, mechanical repairs and woodworking factories, a geological technical school, service facilities, schools, kindergartens, and infant-care centers have been built—in short, Bodaybo is a typical Soviet city.

## Scientific Investigations of Lake Baykal

Anton Chekhov wrote: "Lake Baykal is remarkable, and not for nothing do the Siberian people give him the title of 'sea' and not of 'lake.' The water is unusually transparent, so that it is possible to see through it as through air; it is of a pale turquoise color, which is pleasant to the eye. The banks are mountainous, covered with forests."

This is how Lake Baykal appears to the passenger on the Trans-Siberian Line after an hour's journey from Irkutsk. The train climbs through a mountain pass and crawls into Andrianovka Station, perched on the highest point of the ridge. A panorama of blue water and coastal rocks spreads out below. Then the train begins its descent from the pass along the serpentine of railroad track, winds between volcanic mounds, and eventually emerges at their base. The next stop is Slyudyanka, on the very shore of Lake Baykal. Its name comes from the mica[24] that is mined here, a special sort of mica called *phlogopite*.

In the whole world, there is no other lake as deep as Lake Baykal. Its maximum depth is 1620 meters! The lake is 632 kilometers long and from 25 to 80 kilometers wide. In surface area, it is close to 32,000 square kilometers (larger than the territory of Belgium). The lake contains 23,000 cubic kilometers of water, i.e., one-tenth of all world resources of fresh water. More than 300 rivers flow into Lake Baykal. A complete change of water in the lake takes place every 332 years.

Baykal water is cold even in summer time. Its temperature never rises above 8° Celsius. This is because the upper layers of the water, which are warmed by the sun, "flow" out of the lake into the Angara, at the very mouth of which a stone ridge along the river bottom prevents the flow of cold water from the depth of the lake. People can swim only in places far from the mouth of the Angara, where the water is seasonably warm in summer.

And how to explain the astonishing transparency of the water? For the water is so clear that in spring, when the lake frees itself from its icy armor, a white metallic disk lowered into the lake can be seen at a depth of 40 meters.

Scientists explain the purity of Baykal water not only by its continuous complex physical and chemical processes, but also by the activity of plant and animal organisms. Tiny water plants assimilate mineral and organic substances from the water and during the process of photosynthesis give off a huge quantity of oxygen

[24] *Slyuda*: mica.

which actively influences the decomposition of organic matter. In this way, Lake Baykal undergoes a self-cleansing process.

According to biologists' estimates, there are up to 3 million specimens of a tiny crab, *epishura,* beneath every square meter of lake surface. In search of food—seaweed and bacteria—the epishura draws in and strains water. Moving along a vertical line, the tiny crab consumes everything in its way. At the bottom of the lake, there are only clean stones and sand.

The water of Lake Baykal is very "soft," with four to five times less silicon than the rivers which flow into it. This mineral is extracted from the water by diatomaceous seaweed, which builds its skeleton from it. As it dies, the seaweed sinks to the ground. Without such biological filtration, the silicon contents in Lake Baykal would have been the same as that of its tributaries.

Lake Baykal is peaceful and friendly when the weather is calm. But it is violent and dangerous in a storm. The *Sarma* wind is particularly fierce. It rushes in from the northwest at a speed of more than 60 meters per second and sweeps away everything. The narrow and extended basin of the lake, hemmed in between high mountains, and the river valleys in the coastal ridges all exert an influence on the direction of air currents. Actually, these winds are called after the rivers. Many songs have been composed about Lake Baykal, and in many, the wind *Bargusin* is mentioned. This wind causes turbulence on the water which is dangerous even for large vessels. The *Angarka* blows from the north, from the mouth of the Upper Angara. The *Kultuk* blows from the southwest, usually bringing rainy weather.

Bad or stormy weather, however, is not frequent on Lake Baykal. In summer many tourists who love the sun, the pure air, and the clear water come here. With its many sunny days, the lake's coast is as good as the Mediterranean's. There is an abundance of beautiful bays and beaches and many wooded areas along its shores. The lake is sometimes referred to as "alpine," for good reason: Lake Baykal is situated at a much greater altitude than the well-known Lake Geneva in Switzerland.

Many therapeutic mineral springs dot the coastline. Some of these are hot. The water of the resort Goryachinsk is famous for providing effective relief from rheumatism, gout, neuralgia, and skin problems. A wonderful strip of forest has been preserved in Goryachinsk, between the resort and the golden sand of the beach. Those who come for a rest like to go for walks there. Beneath the crowns of the powerful conifers, the air is filled with the fragrance of gum resin and is particularly clean and pleasant.

Peschannaya[25] Bay, at the foot of the Primorskiy mountain range, is famed for its beach of fine-grained sand and its picturesque landscape. Tourists and holiday-makers come to admire the dark gray, fantastically shaped rocks of the Bolshoy Kolokolnyy and Malyy Kolokolnyy Cliffs. A rare natural phenomenon grows along the banks of the bay: trees "on stilts." Long, straight roots reaching deep into the ground support the pines and larches like stilts. An adult can pass beneath the trunk of the tree without touching it. This is how it

[25] Sandy.

happens: for decades the wind blows the earth out from underneath the trees, while the roots continue to grow downward. In fact, it is not the tree which rises on its roots, but the ground which "sinks."

Bargusinskaya Bay was formed where the river of that name flows into the lake. It boasts a magnificent forest and wonderful views of Lake Baykal. Since the bay is comparatively shallow, the water warms up well.

The water in Krutaya Bay is warmer still, and swimmers can also bathe in Chivyrkuyskaya Bay. There are many rest homes and tourist places on Lake Baykal, in particular, in the city of Baykalsk (southern coast) and along Peschannaya Bay.

There are 22 islands on the lake, the largest among which is Olkhon. It is situated almost in the center of the lake and has an area of 730 square kilometers. Olkhon is inhabited by fishermen. Herds of sheep graze on its meadows. The deepest spot in the lake has been registered not far from the island.

The breeding grounds of the Baykal seal—the *nerp*—which lives only here can be found among the coastal rocks of the Ushanskiye Islands. The nerp has a wonderful coat that is uniform in color and excellent in its durability. In addition, nerp oil is suitable for food.

Rare trees are found on the islands: birches with dark bark, pine trees with considerably thickened trunks near the bottom, aspen trees with unusually shaped leaves.

Baykal fauna are equally unusual. The deepwater fish *golomyanka* (draconculus) is found only in Lake Baykal. A scaleless fish, it is pink in color and consists almost entirely of fat which is valued highly as a healing remedy in Tibetan medicine. It is biologically of interest because it belongs to a species of viviparous fish.

The *omul*,[26] another unique fish, tastes unusually tender and pleasant. Because the stocks of this fish have become depleted, measures have been taken to replenish their numbers. The extent of omul fishing has been restricted and large fish hatcheries have been set up to breed and annually release into the lake tens of millions of this valuable small fish.

The Limnological Institute of the Siberian Department of the Academy of Sciences conducts studies of the lake itself, its geology, fauna, etc. The Institute, located in the village of Listvianka on the southwest bank of the lake, maintains its own fleet of vessels equipped for scientific research, among them the unique laboratory ship *A. Y. Vereshchagin*. The Institute also possesses an industrial workshop and a museum.

The Moscow Institute of Oceanology of the Academy of Sciences, the Limnological Institute, and several other scientific groups carried out combined research on Lake Baykal in the summer of 1977. The scientists made use of small submarines, *Pisces* subs, designed by Soviet experts and constructed in Vancouver, Canada.

The aim of the expedition was to examine the structure of the Baykal "cavity" and determine whether it was similar to the structure of the oceanic rifts (fractures in the crust of the earth). Throughout the summer, the scientists made 42 dives with *Pisces I* and

[26] A kind of salmon.

*Pisces II.* Sightings, photography, and geophysical surveys were carried out. The maximum depth to which the *Pisces* was submerged was 1,410 meters.

The director of the Institute of Oceanology, academician Andrei Monin, explained after the completion of the expedition: "In the course of the experiments we succeeded, for the first time, in clarifying the dynamics of the sedimentary strata, which had accumulated during the 20 to 40 million years of the fracture's existence. It was revealed that their thickness was not less than two kilometers. Hydrobiologists pointed out that the population of Lake Baykal was not all that small in number. At all levels, fish, worms, and crab-like creatures were observed.

"In the final reckoning, we approach the problems of searching for useful minerals. The Baykal zone is rich in various valuable minerals. Having understood the connection between their location and the origin of the fracture, we shall learn how to predict the position of the respective minerals."

Thus, scientists continue to probe the mysteries of Lake Baykal. One thing is certain: this lake is the only gigantic laboratory of its kind, in which the secrets of the movement of the earth's core and the evolution of animal forms are revealed. Here, too, the effect on the natural environment of changes taking place on the shores of the lake is observed. The natural environment of the lake must be preserved inviolate—that is the policy of the Soviet government. At the same time, however, there is no reason not to utilize the tremendous water resources of Lake Baykal for the needs of man. That is the direction in which scientific research is proceeding.

At present, guidelines for the creation and preservation of a Baykal National Park are being elaborated, with the assistance of scientists. In the meantime, any industry producing harmful effluents or other wastes which would pollute the environment has been prohibited along the shores of Lake Baykal.

A sanctuary has been in existence for a long time on the slopes of the Bargusinskiy Ridge (along the eastern coastline), which includes a portion of the lake itself, 100 kilometers long and three kilometers wide, as well as a coastal area of the same length and 45 to 80 kilometers wide. Here, the natural environment is preserved untouched and scientific observations of the world of animals and plants are conducted.

The so-called Bargusinskiy sable, which grows the best pelt in the world, inhabits the banks of the Bargusin River. Its downy and silky dark brown coat has become a great rarity at international fur auctions. When the sanctuary was established, only 20 to 30 animals were counted in the area. Now, the Bargusinskiy sable is no longer threatened with extinction. The number of animals per square kilometer of taiga has already exceeded the level determined by nature, and sables are leaving the confines of the sanctuary to populate new areas.

# The Road of the Ambassadors

The railroad runs along a narrow terrace pressing close to the water's edge. The steep slopes of the Khamar-Daban Ridge hang, so to speak, above the train. Every now and then, the train dives into tunnels broken through the stone mass. All railroad stations on this section of the line are, at the same time, ports on the lake.

After the train crosses the small Snezhnaya[27] River, which flows into Lake Baykal, the first village it passes in Buryatiya is Vydrino. The population here is small, and it is engaged, almost in its entirety, in servicing the railroad or working in the local timber works.

There are even fewer inhabitants in the next village—Tankhoy. According to the last census they numbered hardly more than 3,000. However, Tankhoy has a large port, through which rail cargoes pass, directed along Lake Baykal.

Myssovaya follows and, close to it, the town of Babushkin, named in memory of Lenin's companion-in-arms, the revolutionary Ivan Babushkin. Czarist executioners shot the brave Bolshevik at the railroad depot, without trial or investigation. An obelisk has been erected to mark the site.

Had the train stopped in Boyarskoye and remained there a while, passengers would have had an opportunity to leave the coaches, and, going back a little along the tracks, to climb one of the volcano mounds of the Khamar-Daban foothills. From there, they would have seen a unique panorama of the freshest, cleanest, and apparently endless waterscape and rocks overgrown with trees. And a majestic calm. In the midst of the silence in the foothills of Khamar-Daban it is simply unbelievable that somewhere life goes on, factories work, and cars speed past.

[27] Snowy.

Beyond Boyarskoye, the railroad tracks begin to move away from Lake Baykal, crossing the Bolshaya[28] River, a tributary of the lake. The Bolshaya was apparently named as a joke, for this river is quite narrow and shallow.

Near the mouth of the Bolshaya is the ancient village of Possolsk. In previous centuries, Russian ambassadors traveling to Asian countries used to stop here. The ambassadors usually went by water from Irkutsk, upstream along the Angara, crossed Lake Baykal to Possolsk, stayed there for the night, and in the morning proceeded overland. Possolsk is mentioned, for example, in the papers of ambassadors Fyodor Baikov (1656) and Ivan Perfilyev (1675), and in those of many other representatives of Russia in China. Ambassador Nikolai Spafary (1633-1708) left three manuscripts in which he described in detail his journeys through Siberia to China and told about the significance of Possolsk in those days.

The train moves ahead steadily and the distance from Lake Baykal becomes greater and greater. It travels along the Kudarinskaya Plain where plowed and sowed fields are visible, past Kamensk, near which are major construction works. The train speeds toward Ulan Ude, capital of Buryatiya (Buryat Autonomous Soviet Socialist Republic).

The railroad to the People's Republic of Mongolia starts from Zaudinskaya (eight kilometers along the Trans-Siberian Railroad from Ulan Ude), moves along the right bank of the Selenga River, and then crosses over to the left bank. It continues further along the west

[28] The Great One.

bank of Gussinoye Lake (which is 25 kilometers long and 5-8 kilometers wide).

Near the northern shore of the lake lies the village of Gussinoosersk where up to 4,000 million tons of high-calorie brown coal are mined. The Gussinoosersk mines account for almost 90% of all coal mining in Buryatiya. The coal seams come up to the surface and the mining is inexpensive. A thermoelectric power station is being built in the area.

The Decembrists (the reader has already been told about them) Michael and Nikolai Beztouzhev and Konstantin Torson lived in exile in the village of Staroselenginsk, not far from Gussinoosersk. These people studied the history and economy of Buryatiya and helped the local inhabitants to acquire at least an elementary education.

In 1854, in the *Natural Science Messenger*, a journal published in St. Petersburg, Nikolai Beztouzhev wrote: "In spite of all the impeding circumstances, the Buryat is intelligent . . . the spirit of observation is developed in him to the highest degree . . . As for the mental capacity of the Buryats, they are, in my opinion, equal to all the best races of humanity."

Nikolai Beztouzhev also published articles on the economic and legal situation of the Buryats as well as that of the Russian exiles.

## *Buryatiya*

The Buryat Autonomous Soviet Socialist Republic has an area of 351,300 square kilometers. It is a mountainous country with some grassy plains interspersed. Anton Chekhov called Buryatiya a mixture of Switzerland and the Russian steppes of the Don.

The Buryats formed a nation from Mongol ethnic groups, as well as from local Tungus and Tiurk tribes. Seeking protection against the incursions of hostile neighbors, the Buryat tribes voluntarily began to integrate with Russia at the beginning of the seventeenth century. This process was completed by 1659.

The traditional occupation of the Buryats was animal breeding. They bred cows, sheep, and horses, moving about with their herds within the confines of their *ulus*—a territorial unit. Nominally, the land belonged to all its inhabitants, but, in reality, it was at the disposal of the wealthy cattle breeders and gentry—the *noyons*.

The Russians brought agriculture to Buryatiya. Gradually, not only the Russian elements of civilization but also the Russian spirit of rebellion infiltrated the life of the Buryats. When the first Russian revolution began in 1905, the Buryats also participated in it. The Czar's punitive detachments dealt cruelly with the rebels, but the defeat strengthened their drive for victory during the Socialist revolution.

Today, the former nomads have a developed industry which contributes three-quarters of the total production of the national economy of the Republic. Metallurgy of non-ferrous metals and machine-building, electrotechnical, and instrument-making industries have arisen. Buryatiya exports the products of these industries to 40 foreign countries.

Many varieties of useful minerals are mined in the Republic, including gold, alumina, apatite, wolfram, and molybdenum. New factories are built on this basis. The timber industry is also being developed; the Selenginskiy cellulose and cardboard complex has joined the ranks of enterprises currently in operation.

Although the Buryats learned long ago how to grow corn, vegetables, and potatoes, and although agricultural production is increasing, animal breeding still remains the leading branch of the rural economy of the Republic. It accounts for three-quarters of the total value of the produce of fields and pastures. Large-horned cattle and horses are still bred in Buryatiya, but special attention is given to fine wool sheep breeding. Thousands of silver foxes and mink of various colors are bred on the animal farms.

The Buryat people have acquired a new life in the Soviet era, creating their own fine literature and their own musical art. The novels of the Buryat writers Kh. Namsarayev and Zh. Tumunov have been printed in more than one edition in the various languages of the peoples of the Soviet Union. Despite progress, catching up to and, in some respects, overtaking peoples of a higher cultural level, the Buryats have preserved their own characteristics and their traditions. The ancient art of bone and stone carving, as well as embossing in metal, continues to be practiced. The Buryats are also great masters in the making of adornments for female national costumes.

They do not forget their ancient choral and other dances. As of old, whole ulus come together in the so-called *nadans*—sports gatherings.

The capital of the Republic occupies a favorable geographic position. Ulan Ude sprang up between the

Selenga and Uda Rivers, which merge within the city almost at right angles to each other. The glass works stand here. The closer to the center of the city, the higher the streets rise. The Square of the Soviets, the architectural center of Ulan Ude, is raised above the rest of the city. It was built in Soviet times and consists of many different institutions and multistory buildings in modern architectural style.

Since the 1930's, widespread construction of industrial enterprises has been taking place in the Buryat capital. A locomotive and coach repair works, a major meat works and cannery, a fine cloth mill, the "Electromashina" and "Teplopribor" works, a factory casting reinforced concrete products, a timber-processing plant and food industry undertakings have grown up on the outskirts of the city.

New blocks and streets take shape every year in Ulan Ude. The boundaries of the city have been extended, until now they merge with the industrial districts on the outskirts. In the east, the city has stretched as far as Zaudinskaya Station on the Trans-Siberian Line.

The Buryat Branch of the Siberian Department of the Academy of Sciences and various scientific research institutions have been established in Ulan Ude, where, until 1917, it was difficult to find one literate Buryat. The city, with a population of 308,000, boasts four institutions of higher education, numerous schools, and four theatres, among them the National Theatre of Opera and Ballet.

There is something memorable about Buryatiya. Perhaps it is the contradictory character of its natural environment. Cold, fast rivers with high water levels and stormy rapids share the countryside with peaceful meadows. Herds of sheep, cows, and horses browse alongside the railroad, watched by shepherds (among whom are many women) on horseback. The villages, called *aymaks* here, are fenced by wattle hedges to keep the cattle from wandering. Generally the houses are new and well-built. The exotic *yourts*[29] have long receded into the past.

In the north, the traveler comes to quite a different Buryatiya. It is a country of steep mountain slopes, rocks, and dark, somber pine forests. It is cold and silent. The population density is often one person per 10 square kilometers. Here and there, small Russian and Evenk villages appear in the river valleys.

The Buryats of these districts hunt the famous Siberian sables, squirrels, foxes, and other fur animals on extensive hunting grounds secured for the use of the collective enterprises. The hunters receive from them the necessary equipment, food, ammunition, and medicine, and are taken by helicopter to hunting cabins where they live throughout the entire hunting season, usually two or three to a cabin. From time to time, the helicopters return to replenish the hunters' supplies. The animals are usually hunted in winter, when their fur is particularly dense and firm. In spring, the helicopters bring the hunters home.

While we had a look at the north of Buryatiya, the *Russia* express has crossed the eastern border of this autonomous republic.

---

[29] Huts similar to Indian wigwams.

# What Is Permafrost?

The Eastern Zabaykalye lies along the watershed of the Yenisey, Lena, and Amur systems. All the rivers of the Eastern Zabaykalye are winding and contain rapids. All are thus badly suited for navigation. In winter, most of the rivers freeze down to the bottom. There are several hundred lakes in the Zabaykalye: mountain lakes in the north, and saline lakes in the south.

More than half of the Zabaykalye is covered by the taiga, while steppes stretch out in the south and southeast.

The population of the Zabaykalye (which consists, in the main, of Buryatiya and the Chita Region) comprises a little more than 2 million people; of these, 90 percent are Russians. Among the Russians live Buryats, Evenks, Ukrainians, Tartars, and others. The bulk of the population is concentrated along the Trans-Siberian Railroad.

Mining for the ore of non-ferrous metals and tin smelting has been undertaken in the Zabaykalye. A lumber industry has also been developed.

Agricultural production is limited to sheep breeding. In winter and summer, the sheep are fed on green fodder. In the north the rural population is engaged in deer breeding. Hunting fur animals is also organized in the Zabaykalye.

The first major station on the Trans-Siberian Line in the Eastern Zabaykalye is called Petrovskiy Zavod.[30]

---

[30] Petrovsky Works.

It adjoins the city of Petrovsk-Zabaykalskiy, which evolved from a settlement of workers from the cast iron works founded in 1789. The iron ore obtained in the vicinity was remelted in the works. Although the reserves of the local raw material turned out to be small, metallurgic production was not relinquished. Moreover, a new plant was built side by side with the old in 1939-1940. It utilizes the waste of black metals for the smelting of steel in open-hearth furnaces.

Petrovsk-Zabaykalskiy stretches along the railroad in narrow river valleys between the mountain ridges. The train track comes so close to the walls of the plant that the open-hearth furnaces, with their flames raging above, can be seen from the windows of the coaches. The city also has a glass works and a meat works. However, considering its population figure, Petrovsk-Zabaykalskiy is not large.

The city is famous because it was here that the progressives of Russia were subjected to the Siberian *katorga*[31]—the Decembrists, the Polish patriots struggling for the independence of their homeland against the Czar's autocracy, and the revolutionary democrats.

It was in Petrovsk-Zabaykalskiy, too, that the builders of the Trans-Siberian Line encountered an insidious feature of nature. Brick buildings—including the depot, the workshops, and the forge—began to fall into ruin at a great pace and for unknown reasons. The builders searched for causes for a long time. Only additional failures and wide-ranging research uncovered the true "enemy" of building in these places—permafrost.

Frozen ground in and around Petrovsk-Zabaykal-

[31] Hard labor.

skiy occurs only in the form of separate islands in an area of 10 to 40 square meters. The railroad builders learned to by-pass the islands of permafrost. Where this was not possible, they resorted to artificially induced thawing of the frozen ground—a very labor-consuming and costly procedure.

Along the tracks beyond Petrovsk-Zabaykalskiy, ordinary telegraph poles are set in peculiar wooden "baskets" filled with stones. This is how the swelling of the ground is combatted. Any pole sunk shallowly into the ground in the zone of permafrost would creep out a little every year. In winter, the upper layer of the ground freezes to the depth of permafrost while increasing in volume. As a result, the surface of the ground lifts 10 to 20 centimeters. A pole would lift up with the ground and a cavity would form underneath it. In summer, when the ground thaws for some depth and drops, the pole could not return to its previous position because the cavity beneath would have been filled by crumbling earth. After a few years, the pole would "jump out" of the ground.

The swelling of the ground is one of the problems which make the construction of railroads and highways difficult in Eastern Siberia. Permafrost "tears" concrete and asphalt, and leads to the collapse of buildings and track. Soviet scientists and builders are coming closer to a complete solution to the problem of permafrost. Large buildings are not erected on foundations, but on poles sunk deeply into the ground, while particularly dangerous sections of permafrost in the way of railroad and highway construction are scooped out by excavating machines, and the bed of the track or road is refilled with more solid foundation material.

Twenty kilometers southeast of Petrovsk-Zabaykalskiy, the train passes the station of Balyaga. A large lumber complex is situated nearby. A few more kilometers, and it passes Novopavlovka, where brown coal is mined.

Southeast of Novopavlovka, in the valley of the Chikoy River, is Yamarovka, one of the most popular resorts of the Zabaykalye. It has been in operation for more than a hundred years. The pride of the resort is the mineral water which brings relief from many illnesses.

Beyond Petrovsk-Zabaykalskiy, one more resort is built on mineral springs—the sanatorium Kuka, recommended to persons with various stomach and intestinal disorders. The local factory bottling Kukinskaya mineral water has also been in operation for many decades.

The remaining places on this section of the Trans-Siberian Line, between the Petrovskiy Works and Chita—Khushenga, Khorchetoy, Bada, and Magzon— are mainly involved with forest exploitation. Here too, the *Russia* passes the post marking the 6,000th kilometer of the journey.

# Part VI
# Photographs

Dispatch of furs for auction in Leningrad. Photograph by A.P.N.

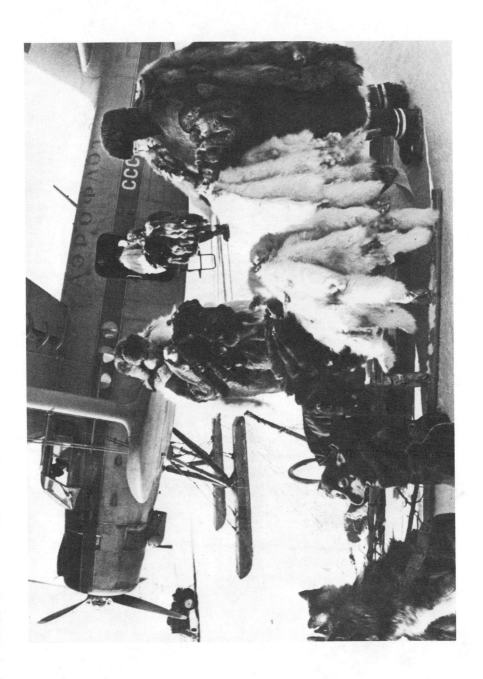

Lake Baykal. Photograph by A. Freyd-berg.

Glimpse of Lake Baykal in winter. Photograph by A. Lekhmus.

Submarine "Pisces XI" used for scientific observations 1400 meters below the surface of Lake Baykal. Photograph by P. Malinovsky.

Lesson at Secondary School of Music at
Ulan Ude. Photograph by V. Reznikov.

Effects of permafrost. Photograph by L.
Weysman.

# Part VII

# From the Capital: 7,000 Kilometers

## The Siberian Cossacks

Chita occupies a favorable position astride the pass across the morose and unfriendly Yablonovyy mountain range. All roads to the Far East from the Zabaykalye lead through Chita. The location of the city was selected as successfully as, for example, that of Sverdlovsk in the Urals. Peter Beketov, an ordinary man who in 1663 built the first shelter, a timber house on the pass, decided by this action where Chita was to be.

Within 200 years, Chita had become the center of the Zabaykalye region and the seat of command of the newly formed Cossack army.

Permit us, dear reader, to digress and explain who the Cossacks were and what part they played in the history of Russia.

*V. Kuranov*

The Russian Cossack community originated in the fifteenth century on the southern outskirts of the European part of the Russian State, as the result of a protest movement of its own kind. Those who were dissatisfied with the actions of the feudal lords, who did not want to pay any more tribute, or who simply wanted to escape from the bondage of serfdom—these people who were against the oppression existing in Russia gathered in the low country of the Dnieper and the Don. Forming themselves into armed bands, they roamed the outskirts of the principalities, sometimes raiding rich caravans and merchant ships. The Cossack ideal was complete personal freedom, elected government, equality of the members of the community, contempt for all privileges, and mutual assistance against external enemies.

At first the Russian government tried to liquidate the Cossack band, sending out punitive detachments against them, but it could not achieve this aim. Finally, the Czar recognized the freedom of the Cossacks and their right to an autonomous government. In their turn, the Cossacks took upon themselves the obligation to defend Russia's borders against plunderers.

During different periods of Russia's history, the Cossacks enjoyed different kinds of independence. At the time of the acquisition of Siberia, the Cossacks had the right of land use in the border zone and self-government. At the same time, they were obligated to present themselves for military duty with their own arms and horses. The service lasted a number of years, after which the Cossacks returned to their rural pursuits. Every year the Cossacks appeared for a muster; in the event of war, the entire male population of every Cossack village had to

turn out against the enemy. Czarist military command-
ers used to select detachments of shock troops from
among the Cossacks who were experienced and used to
the hardships of life in the field.

The Cossacks were subdivided into Volga, Don,
Ural, Orenburg, and Siberian Cossacks, depending on
the district of settlement. A large territory inhabited by
Cossacks was called a "Cossack Army." The name and
size of the "Army" often changed in accordance with the
Czar's will.

Most of the Siberian pioneers were descended from
Cossacks. Small groups of these bold, freedom-loving
people made difficult and complicated expeditions into
the depths of completely unknown lands, establishing
business relationships with the indigenous tribes and, if
necessary, defending them against stronger and hostile
neighbors. The Cossacks built their own forts (*ostrogi*)
far from home and very often had no contact with their
native villages for years. The independent Cossacks
understood the feelings of other people and developed a
mutual understanding with them.

After the October Revolution the Cossacks lost their
privileged position.

Among the Zabaykalye Cossacks, whose center in
the nineteenth century became Chita, were Russians as
well as people of different Siberian tribes and people of
mixed descent. They were distinguished by a comparatively dark complexion, great physical endurance, and
Siberian simplicity and artlessness.

The Zabaykalye Cossacks laid the foundations of
most of the present villages in this particular district.
Later they continued to build and extend them. On the

new lands they began to sow corn and grow vegetables, passing on their agricultural experience to the indigenous people.

# Chita

A new stage in the development of Chita began in 1900 when the tracks of the Trans-Siberian Line reached the city. Chita happened to be on the intersection of two transport routes to the Far East and to China. Major railroad workshops, locomotive depots, a flour mill, a saw mill, and a brick factory arose here. Mining of coal was begun to satisfy the needs of the line.

During the first Russian revolution of 1905, Chita workers and soldiers, led by the Bolsheviks, took power in the city, and along the whole Zabaykalskaya Railroad.

The "Chita Republic" was born and the publication of *Zabaykalskiy Rabochiy*,[32] one of the first workers' papers in the country, was started. However, the Czar crushed the Chita Republic in the most cruel manner: the leaders of the workers' committee and active participants in the revolutionary movement were taken to the base of the Titovskaya volcanic mound and shot. A monument has been erected on that spot.

Contemporary Chita is a regional center. Its population figure exceeded the 200,000 mark long ago. The central districts of the city are formed by a number of parallel streets which follow the contours of the volcanic mound one above the other. The upper roads have already reached the pine forest. This is where the television center has been built.

[32] Zabaykal Worker.

The main square of Chita is Lenin Square, framed by the substantial building of the Administration of the Zabaykalskaya Railroad, the Hotel Zabaykalye, the twin movie theatres "Rodina,"[33] the buildings of the City Committee of the Communist Party and the Council of People's Deputies, and the ancient building of the post office.

The Chernovskiy District of Chita is considered to be a miner's district. Here are the homes of the miners who work on the nearby brown coal fields.

In Chita there are numerous monuments to the past, among them the "Decembrists Church." The name came from the fact that it stood not far from the barracks where the Decembrists languished from 1827 to 1830. In this church, in 1827, the Frenchwoman Polina Gebel was wedded to the Decembrist Ivan Annenkov. She was not afraid to become the wife of a "state criminal," a convict, although the price of this union was the loss of her freedom and her civil and property rights.

The church had been built from thick larch logs in 1776; the ceiling is supported by an arch and columns. Larch lumber is almost impervious to rot, even when directly on the ground. Only after it had stood for a hundred years was a stone foundation laid under the church.

To the attractions of Chita should be added Lake Kenon, a favorite summer recreation spot of the citizens. Seven kilometers long and up to three kilometers wide, the lake is deep and originates from a spring.

The Pedagogic and Medical Institutes and several other institutes in Irkutsk and in other cities of the Soviet

[33] Motherland.

Union have opened branch facilities in Chita in Soviet times. Of the scientific institutions, mention should be made of the Zabaykalskiy Combined Scientific Research Institute, the Economics and Geography Laboratories, as well as the Forest Economy Laboratory of the Siberian Department of the Academy of Sciences.

The air in Chita and its surroundings is very pure and dry, and a great many days are sunny. This perhaps explains why, in the countryside around the city, there are many resorts and sanatoria.

Sixty-two kilometers from Chita, the *Russia* express passes through Darasun Station. In the village there is a mining equipment factory and an important motor highway, Chita-Khapcheranga (a border town on the Soviet Mongolian border) passes through.

Darasun is famed for its sanatoria, near carbonic mineral springs, where hypertonia and cardiovascular, intestinal, and abdominal ailments are treated. The healing water of Darasun has been exported to China and Korea since ancient times.

The next station is Tarskaya. From here a railroad runs to Peking, Pyonyang, and Hanoi.

## The River Shilka: A Wonderful Landscape and Dredges for Gold

As it passes through the Zabaykalye, the Trans-Siberian Railroad runs for a considerable distance along the banks of the Rivers Ingoda and Shilka. The Shilka flows through a mountainous and mostly forest-clad valley between the ridges. The mountains break off fairly steeply near the water and the railroad bed literally "molds itself" against the steep inclines, as if trying to repeat all the turns of the capricious river.

The train approaches Shilka, a young town which originated as a small station settlement in 1897 but did not gain the privileges of a town until 1951. A number of enterprises engaged in servicing and repairing railroad transport, as well as in processing agricultural raw materials, are concentrated in Shilka.

North of Shilka a highway leads to the village of Vershino-Darasunskoye. Many thousands of years ago, a volcano was active here. Then it became extinct and eventually it disintegrated under the action of the sun, wind, and water. Layers containing gold became visible inside the crater, and gradually the gold was washed away by rivers and rivulets which carried it into the valleys. Legend has it that a hunter accidentally came to one of the springs. He noticed grains of a shiny metal, started to collect these in his cap, and filled it to the brim. That is why the gold field in Vershino-Darasun-skoye is named Usur-Malakhay, which, translated from the local language, means "golden hat."

Still further north, on the same highway, lies the village of Usugli, where fluoric spar, a mineral essential in chemistry and metallurgy, is extracted. A local hunter found the deposits in 1954, and that is not a legend. A hunter by the name of Sobolev was stalking a fox which took refuge in a burrow. Looking into the burrow, Sobolev saw an unusual purple and green stone. When he showed his find to geologists, it turned out to be a major deposit. The extraction of fluoric spar has been conducted here ever since.

South of Shilka lies the resort Shivanda (translated from the local language this means "royal drink"). The resort has been in existence for almost a hundred years, and its mineral water helps in the healing of many ailments.

Forty-five kilometers east of Shilka, the train will pass Priiskovaya[34] Station. The settlement here is small, with fewer than 2,000 inhabitants. From here the highway leads to the gold mining center of Baley. The gold prospecting district lies south of the Trans-Siberian Line beyond the Borshchovochnyy mountain range. In the beginning, auriferous sand was washed here, but in the 1920's auriferous quartz veins were found. The first gold from these ores was obtained in 1929. Today, gold is obtained in Baley from both auriferous sand and auriferous ore.

Between Baley and Priiskovaya Station, at a height of 850 meters above sea level, the resort Urguchan has been built in the river valley. Its therapeutic features include an unusually favorable local climate and carbonated mineral water springs.

From Priiskovaya Station a rail line six kilometers long branches off and goes north to Nerchinsk, the oldest town of the Zabaykalye. Founded in 1658, it once was an important administrative and political center, but its significance dwindled after the construction of the Trans-Siberian Railroad. Today, Nerchinsk is the administrative center of an agricultural district.

Left from the past are the rows of shops, built of stone, in the central square and a palace built in Moorish

[34] *Priisk*: mine.

style by the gold prospector Bautin, in the last century. Shops still occupy the old building in the central square, while the palace has been taken over by a movie, a music school, and the municipal library.

After passing Kuenga Station, the line turns sharply north, leaving the Shilka Valley. It is generally recognized that the banks of the Ingoda, a tributary of the Shilka—as well as the banks of Shilka itself—are the most beautiful places on the whole journey from Moscow to Vladivostok. Of course, these beauties of nature cannot be seen from the coach window. If, however, the passenger could manage to take a walking tour or a drive along the Shilka, he would never forget the unique panoramas of the Siberian landscape. With each turn of the river a new landscape appears, a new harmonious blend of trees, grass, flowers, rocks, and water.

The village of Chernyshevsk comes next, named in memory of the revolutionary democrat Nikolai Chernyshevskiy (1828-1889), who spent long years at hard labor in the Nerchinsk region. The villagers here are mainly engaged in work connected with the railroad.

Past Chernyshevsk (more accurately called Chernyshevsk-Zabaykalskiy), the climb up the Amur mountain range begins. At the top, the railroad again changes direction and turns northeast. Without stopping, the train passes Busheley, where molybdenum ore deposits have been found and where a large mineral enrichment plant is under construction. From the train window, passengers may possibly see a dredge digging for gold in the Chornyy Uryum River. Such dredges also operate on the tributaries of this river. The prospectors live near the stations which flash by the train window: Ksenyevskaya,

Mostovka, Chaldon and others. The railroad rises to the next ridge, past stations with names like Tyazhelyy[35] and Perevalnyy,[36] and goes through Razdolnaya beyond it.

The last major inhabited place within the Zabaykalye is Mogocha, in the vally of the River Bolshoy Amazar. It began as a workers' settlement during the construction of the railroad. The bases and stores of geological research expeditions working in the northern districts, as well as those of the gold prospecting enterprises and mines, are concentrated here. The exploration of the Zabaykal North also originates from Mogocha.

Mogocha is almost devoid of vegetation, and its wooden houses look black. The culprits are permafrost and the sun. In winter, the thermometer can register close to 60° Celsius below zero, while in summer the sun literally turns the wooden structures to charcoal and burns off grass and hedges.

Mogocha belongs to those districts where it is hard to live and work, yet people *do* live and work there—and learn and dream and love. Men can do anything. Involuntarily, that thought enters the mind of the traveler on this line.

## A Little Geography of the Far East

Soviet geographers and economists call "Far East" that huge territory of the Soviet Union (an area of more than 3 million square kilometers) that is bounded by the River

---

[35] Heavy one.
[36] *Pereval*: mountain pass.

Amur in the south, by the Stanovoy mountain range in the west and by the Pacific Ocean in the east. Of the eleven time zones of the Soviet Union, five are in the Far East.

The Trans-Siberian Railroad crosses into the Soviet Far East when it enters the Amur Region, a subzone of light (larch) pine woods and relatively mild climate. It is the main granary of the Far East. The train moves on to the Khabarovskaya Territory, a zone of dark pine woods and a moderately harsh climate. The region is considered the industrial heartland of the Far East. From the city of Khabarovsk, the train turns almost due south and heads into the Maritime Territory, with its pine and broad-leafed woods and mild climate. The Primorye[37] is the region of sailors, fishermen, and industrial workers, although agriculture is also well-developed.

Mountains and *sopki*[38] take up three-quarters of the Far East and form the Pacific Ocean ore-belt containing the richest deposits of gold, tin, wolfram, lead, mercury, and many other useful minerals. Among the volcanoes is one of the highest on earth—the Kliuchevskaya Sopka (4,750 meters).

The region is distinguished by a remarkable variety and rare blending of the flora and fauna of the south with that of the north: the northern pine grows side by side with the southern liana and wild grape, and the path of the northern stag is also used by that southern predator—the tiger.

From ancient times, the indigenous people of the Far East have had their own literature and their own

[37] Another name for the Maritime Territory.
[38] *Sopka*: a small extinct volcano.

original art. Some magnificent sculptures, traces of the high cultural development of the indigenous population, have been found in the Priamurye, in a cave not far from Vladivostok. The ancient and medieval civilization of the Far East had a local base. The Tungus tribes were independent and had their own powerful states. In the seventh century, they were already engaged in agriculture, like peasants in other countries of the world.

The ties between the people of European Russia and those of Siberia and the Far East go back into distant centuries, and when Siberia and the Far East became part of Russia, it was, as it were, a culmination of ancient and profound economic processes. Such was the objective necessity, conditioned by the very course of history.

From the point of view of economic progress, the Far East is the most dynamic section of the country. Its industry grows four times faster than the corresponding average growth throughout the U.S.S.R., and the population density is also steadily increasing. In the coming years, the Far East, like the rest of the country, is expected to continue to realize even more of its economic potential.

## The North of the Amur Region

There are no large cities along the Great Railroad in the Amur Region. The line runs through the harsh region of the mountainous north, where there are few inhabitants, and these are mainly employed in servicing the railroad. Some work in the gold mines and some have been engaged in lumbering in recent years.

The first station signficant according to local standards which the express train passes in the Amur Region is called Yerofey Pavlovich. Situated on the bank of the River Urka, it was named after the Russian traveler Yerofey Pavlovich Khabarov who, back in the seventeenth century, came through these places on the way to the Amur. Near the station, a kilometer post is marked 7,000—the distance from the Capital.

The climate of the district adjoining this section of the railroad is hard to live with. The frosts last almost from the middle of October to the beginning of April. The average January temperature is 33° below zero and sometimes the temperature is far below 50° below zero. In winter, mists can be observed, while the air crackles when one exhales rapidly: the steam from the human mouth instantly turns into ice, the crystals of which explode with a light snap.

Ice forms often in these places during cold weather; ground water comes up to the surface where it freezes. During particularly heavy frosts and bright sunshine, steam rises above the ice. Sometimes this ice remains until the middle of July in the form of ice "hats" in the midst of green grass.

Two hundred kilometers further east, the train reaches Skovorodino—a community of railroad workers and the most northern town of the Amur Region. A scientific research station investigating permafrost operates here. The city has been named in memory of the first president of the village council of workers' deputies, A. N. Skovorodin.

Skovorodino is a rail junction. From here a line branches south along the Bolshoy Never River to the

Amur. Villages of lumberjacks have sprung up quite recently at the 19th and 50th kilometers along this line.

Sixteen kilometers east of Skovorodino is Bolshoy Never, which may be called a gateway of its own kind to the gold mines of Aldan and into Yakutiya. The Amur-Yakutiya road starts here. "Motor trains" weighing many tons (motor trucks with several cargo trailers attached) circulate in an unending stream in both directions on this road. Let us also undertake a journey on it.

# Part VII
# Photographs

Dredge operating at Baley gold mines.
Photograph by G. Kalachyan.

# Part VIII
# Present Distance—8,533 Kilometers from Moscow

## Camel Caravans in Yakutiya

A road sign at the pass over the Stanovoy mountain range, where the highway takes us from Bolshoy Never, reads: "Yakutskaya A.S.S.R.[39] 379 kilometers to Aldan" and on the reverse side, "Amur Region, 269 kilometers to Bolshoy Never."

The surrounding mountains are bare or covered with stunted growth. The thick forests have ended; no more spreading, elegant birches. A considerable amount of material for road construction, as well as for the Aldan gold mines, was supplied by camel caravans when the section of road from Bolshoy Never to Aldan was built in 1926-1931. A paradox: southern animals and northern frosts.

[39] Autonomous Soviet Socialist Republic of Yakutiya.

Seventeen kilometers from the road sign is the first village on the Yakut side—Nagornyy, where workers from the nearby Lebedinny gold fields live.

Here starts the golden land of Yakutiya. Geographically the Autonomous Soviet Socialist Republic of Yakutiya forms part of Western Siberia. Comprising an area of more than 3 million square kilometers, it is the largest of the autonomous republics of the Soviet Union—and the least populous. Its basic population, the Yakuts, belong to the Tiurk language group of peoples, but their dictionary contains many Mongol and Tungus elements. The Yakuts led a nomadic existence over many centuries, breeding deer, fishing, and hunting. Settlements did not appear in Yakutiya until the seventeenth century.

We are descending now from the Stanovoy Pass. Lonely neglected cabins appear every 20 to 30 kilometers along the road. They are called *budkas* here, and they all have their own names. Some time ago, road rangers lived in them. Today, with the advent of a new and more advanced technology, there is no more need for the rangers, and the budkas stand empty.

The farther from the pass, the more vegetation there is. Mountain tundra gives way, little by little, to taiga. Look to the side of the road. The trees on the stony slope of the hill are peculiarly stooped. The local inhabitants call this "drunken forest." It appears on slopes where "flowing" of the ground occurs: if the slope faces north, frozen, ice-saturated ground stratifies below the surface layer. During the thaw, a layer oversaturated with moisture forms, and the unfrozen earth begins to slide upon it, bending and felling trees.

The road winds between rows of stony hills; there is not a soul around, no wisp of smoke from a dwelling.

And yet, unexpectedly a village appears near the river below. It is named Chulman and stands on the river bank. Smoke rises from a thermoelectric power station. Chulman is the center of the geological expeditions which conduct their exploration over the whole of southern Yakutiya.

We continue further. The rounded summit of the Evot Mountain appears. Colossal deposits of iron ore have been found nearby, in some places so close to the surface that mining can be carried out by the open cut method. Not far away are large deposits of coking coal. A major industrial complex will stand here in the near future. A railroad branching from the Trans-Siberian Line and called by the builders "Little B.A.M." has already been brought to this site.

The Aldan Highland rises behind the Evot Mountain. Somewhere near the Nezametnyy[40] Spring, where the town of Aldan stands today, a hunter named Mikhail Tarabukin found rich gold deposits. Planned systematic exploration of the highland began in 1922-1923. The first dredge was put into operation in 1926. At first supplies for the gold fields were sent along the Lena River, and from there by horses. Up to 50 horses used to be put into harness to transport heavy equipment. Since 1931, however, all transport is taken care of by motor vehicles.

Aldan is situated between two hills. Its houses are of wood, solid and well-constructed. There is much vegetation in the town—poplars are prominent. The poplar did not originally grow in these latitudes, but some unknown amateurs imported it, and the trees became accustomed to the place and grew tall.

[40] Invisible.

*V. Kuranov*

Several villages and various subsidiary enterprises are located around the town. There are even some agricultural state farms. In these harsh parts, people manage to grow potatoes and other vegetables for the gold miners, and supply them with dairy products.

Near Aldan, as in every gold mining district, there are deserted villages. What happens is this: a dredge can work over a strip of ground several hundred meters long in one year; after three or four years, the workers leave the old village and settle in a new one, closer to the dredge.

A few words about the dredge itself. It is called a gold factory. The structure floats on water and is equipped with a conveyor belt with buckets with up to a 250-liter capacity. The buckets scoop up the earth beneath the dredge and pour their contents into a special bunker. A whole battery of shaking trays throws off the rough pieces of broken stone. Then the ore is conveyed to vibrating trays and washed with water. The lighter particles of scooped up earth are carried away, but the gold remains in special recesses.

Apart from gold, the Aldan Highland is rich in mica. The center of the mica industry—Tommot—stands along the highway north of Aldan. Its first building was erected in 1925, but Tommot grew mainly in the post-war years. Signs of the new can be seen in the economic, social, and architectural aspects of the town. The builders also took care of planting: along the streets there are many simple black alder trees; the preserved areas of the taiga within the city have become small parks.

But let us say farewell to distant Yakutiya and

return again to the Siberian Line. The train proceeds from Bolshoy Never to Svobodnyy.

## Amur Black Soil

The city of Svobodnyy is situated on the right bank of the Zeya River. The transfer of goods from the railtrucks of the Trans-Siberian Line to the river cargo vessels takes place here. A highway runs south to Blagoveshchensk and north to Norsk.

Founded in 1912, Svobodnyy is developing as an industrial city: it already features metal working, building of train coaches, and production of spare parts of motor vehicles.

Not far from the city, a fruit nursery supplies saplings of apple, pear, and cherry trees and slips of raspberry and gooseberry bushes to the collective farms of the surrounding area. Gardening penetrates this region under great difficulties, but it does so, nevertheless, gradually.

The plain is the most populated part of the Amur Region, and the agriculture is of significance for the whole region. Amur black soil yields good crops of wheat, barley, rice, soya, watermelons, and other kinds of melons.

The settlements on the Zeysko-Bureinskaya Plain are 10-20 kilometers apart, separated by yellowish fields of barley and dark green fields of soya or broad-leafed plantings of melons and cucumbers. Settlers from Russia live here. Many villages have entered upon the second century of their existence, but their appearance still reflects national characteristics. The Ukrainian villages, for example, can be distinguished by their white-washed *khatas*[41] gleaming in the sun, the Russian villages by their houses of solid log construction with characteristic overlapping of log ends.

It must be noted that the Zeysko-Bureinskaya Plain has been populated by man since time immemorial. This is confirmed by archeological finds. The people who lived here engaged in fishing, hunting, and agriculture.

# Blagoveshchensk: The Frontier Is Near

Blagoveshchensk, the principal city of the Amur Region, is 100 kilometers south of the line, on the very border between the Soviet Union and China. It was founded by Cossacks in 1856. The population increased and the military outpost quickly became a Cossack *stanitza*.[42] A year later, it was a town.

Today Blagoveshchensk has some 177,000 inhabitants. It is laid out like a gridiron, its streets stretching from west to east along the Amur and from south to north parallel to the Zeya River. It is a green and picturesque city where poplars, maples and Siberian pea trees grow along the footpaths. The central avenue bears the name of Lenin. It is flanked by modern multistory residential blocks and administrative buildings.

Blagoveshchensk may be called a city of students. It

---

[41] Peasant huts.
[42] Cossack village.

has pedagogic, agricultural, and medical institutes; a school specializing in river transport, a polytechnical and agricultural college, a college of civil engineering and construction, a building and financial-technical college, and a teachers' college.

The scientific research institutions are represented by the Far Eastern Zonal Veterinary Institute, by the laboratories of the Far Eastern Branch of the Siberian Department of the Academy of Sciences, and by the Blagoveshchensk Latitude Laboratory of the Principal Astronomic Observatory of the Academy of Sciences.

Industry is also developing in Blagoveshchensk. It already produces drilling machines, electrical equipment, asphalt, and concrete constructions. A grain elevator has been erected in the eastern part of the city, and there are several flour mills nearby.

Further on, Zavitaya Station dispatches and receives goods for the relatively small (population about 20,000 people) town of Zavitinsk, chiefly noted for its railroad transport repair shops and a factory that processes soya oil and soya flour.

After 45 kilometers of travel from Zavitaya along the Trans-Siberian Line, the train arrives at Bureya Station, from which a branch line goes southwest to the young town of Raychikhinsk. Coal mining by the open cut method is the main occupation. After powerful excavating machines have removed the topmost layer of soil, a temporary railroad is brought up to the coal seams which are blasted with explosives. The same excavating machines load the pieces of coal into wagons.

Raychikhinsk coal is one of the cheapest in the country. It is delivered first to the thermoelectric power station operating nearby. From here, power is transmitted to Svobodnyy, Belogorsk, Blagdoveshchensk, and many villages of the Zeysko-Bureinskaya Plain. A power line has been installed from Raychikhinsk to the construction site of the Zeyskaya hydroelectric station, which will be the largest in the Far East.

Raychikhinsk serves as the center of a whole group of industrial settlements with a total population of more than 50,000 people. Each settlement originated near an industrial enterprise—a lighting engineering plant, a factory producing prefabricated concrete constructions, a glass works, etc.

In summer, as the *Russia* express approaches the bridge across the Bureya, the pleasant fragrance of flowering linden trees, of fresh meadows and moisture carries through the windows of the coaches. The Khingan State Sanctuary, in which the rich and varied flora and fauna of the Far East are preserved, comes right up to the railroad. Near Arkhara Station, the sanctuary consists of swampy lowlands. Here and there among the untouched overgrowth rise islands of luxurious woods, birch thickets, and groups of maples, with a thick undergrowth of forest hazel nut trees. In places, the lowlands become a *bolotnaya tryassina*, literally a marshy swamp. Shrubs, reeds, and grass form a thick and elastic carpet on which one can walk without breaking through. At every step, the marsh recedes underfoot and then springs up again, so that the effect is of walking on green waves.

The sanctuary is rich in Mongol and Siberian animals seldom encountered elsewhere (raccoon-like dogs, for example, and black bears). Among the many medicinal plants found in the Khingan Sanctuary, the "wild pepper," which is considered the "blood brother" of ginseng, deserves mention. Wild grapes, "Amur-velvet" trees, and Korean cedar pine also grow in the sanctuary.

The Stanovoy Mountains stretch to the north of the railroad for the entire distance that the train travels within the borders of the Amur Region. They extend over 800 kilometers and give the Zeya and other rivers their sources. These mountains have a beauty quite their own. Only the larch can grow on the rocks and stony ground, frozen forever to a great depth. On the gentler slopes, birches hang on by their roots to stony outcroppings. And in the gaps between the rocks grows the *bagulink*[43] a plant which fills the air with intoxicating fragrance.

These not very dense forests are representative of the typical dark coniferous taiga, somewhat morose, somewhat unfriendly, but unusually attractive in its virgin wildness.

The upper mountain slopes are covered with low-growing cedars. This is a remarkable plant. Lower down on the slope, where it borders with larches, the cedar is a conifer about three meters high. The closer to the summit, the smaller the cedar becomes, and on the very summit, where cold winds blow continuously, it turns into crawling undergrowth. No taller than ordinary grass, these plants still produce small cones with oily nuts which local inhabitants use for food. Squirrels, bears, and sables also like to feast on them.

[43] Marsh ledum.

The Zeya Sanctuary is in the eastern part of the Stanovoy mountain range. Sables, wild northern stags, roebucks, elk, musk deer, and numerous birds live here. Especially protected is a bird called *dikousha* which has been close to extinction in the past. It has tasty meat and is completely unafraid of man. No gun is required to hunt this bird. A wooden pole with a string noose at the end is sufficient to pull a dikousha down from a tree.

## The Jewish Autonomous Region

In 1928 the Presidium of the Central Executive Committee of the U.S.S.R. (now the Presidium of the Supreme Soviet of the U.S.S.R.) adopted a resolution to secure the unoccupied territories near the Amur River for voluntary settlement by Jewish workers residing in the U.S.S.R. and abroad. In the summer of that year, the first settlers from the Ukraine and Byelorussia started moving into that region.

The settlers from Mohilev and Dniepropetrovsk (Ukraine) reached the Far East in July, traveling in whole families, together with their livestock and agricultural implements. They stopped in the warm forest, suffused with the fragrance of resin and pines, put up their tents, and founded the village of Waldheim ("home in the forest").

Another group laid the foundations for the first log houses of the village Amurzet—an acronym of "Amurskoye Zemelnoye Yevreiskoye Tovarishchestvo."[44] Later,

---

[44] Amur Jewish Land Association.

the land association was transformed into a *kolkhoz*, the collective farm Amurzet.

Some explanation of what a kolkhoz is: the members of a kolkhoz own their livestock and major agricultural implements in common, i.e., tractors, motor vehicles, combine harvesters, sowing machines, etc. The cooperative also owns the livestock sheds, poultry houses, etc. The members of the kolkhoz work in brigades, and each brigade is engaged in a particular kind of work. Every month, the kolkhoz pays the members a monetary advance toward the future harvest (this money is given to the kolkhoz as a State subsidy). After the harvest has been brought in, the members of the kolkhoz receive a final settlement based on the year's total and on the quantity and quality of the expended work and the extent of the income of the whole cooperative. Part of the income goes toward the extension of the kolkhoz production. Each kolkhoz family has its own home, a small plot of land, livestock, and poultry.

The kolkhoz is managed by the members of the cooperative themselves, who solve the most important questions at general meetings. The meeting elects the management of the kolkhoz and the president, who attend to the business of the cooperative in the period between general meetings, and represent, as it were, executive power. The land is left to the kolkhoz by the State for perpetual use, free of cost.

In the U.S.S.R. there are almost no individual farmers who would till the land with their own hands and at their own risk. In principle, individual land use is permitted by the State. But the collective method of conducting farming has firmly and universally entered into Soviet practice. It raises the efficiency of agricultural production, eases the labor of the peasants, and permits them to make use of different technological means. For only the kolkhoz, with a firm financial base resting on bank credit, is capable of acquiring tractors and combines, cultivators and grain dryers, irrigation installations and motor vehicles. The members of the kolkhoz have no worry about the sale of the harvest either. It is bought by the State. The kolkhoz may invite experienced specialists for permanent work: an animal specialist, an agronomist, an engineer or technician. At present the kolkhoz farms send young members to different schools in the country for advanced education and pay them a stipend during the period of study. Having obtained a diploma, the young specialists return to their native village, to take charge of the animal breeding farm, the field brigade, or the kolkhoz garage.

Hospitals and schools built in the kolkhoz are, as a rule, financed by State grants. But wealthier kolkhoz farms may, by decision of the members of the cooperative, take part in the construction of these buildings with their own means and labor.

All members of the kolkhoz are entitled to a State old-age pension (for women at 55 years of age, for men at 60).

The largest kolkhoz in the Jewish Autonomous Region is Trudovaya Niva,[45] in the village of Waldheim, which has already been mentioned. Today more than 1,500 people live there. Its main street stretches for more than a kilometer. The kolkhoz has a boarding school, a

[45] Labor field

secondary school of general education, its own hospital, a large kolkhoz club, and shops. Each year, the collective sells the state 30,000-35,000 hundredweights of vegetables, up to 40,000 hundredweights of milk, and large quantities of meat, soya, and potatoes. It is hard to imagine that at one time there was a taiga forest here.

The industrial zone of the Jewish Autonomous Region adjoins the Trans-Siberian Railroad, in an area where the climate is somewhat harsher than in the agricultural south. Not far from the town of Obluchye, where our train has already arrived, there are underground workings of deposits of "tin stone"—cassiterite. A miners' settlement, Khingansk, has arisen here. Somewhat further east are iron ore deposits. This is the future base of the black metallurgy of the Far East.

Forty-four kilometers beyond Obluchye is the B.A.M. station. The railroad branch to the future Baykal-Amur Line runs north from here. At the 34th kilometer of this line, between two branches of the Malyy Khingan, is the resort Kuldur. It is said that once an Evenk hunter, pursuing a wounded stag, came to a spring which, in winter, was not frozen. The snow around this spring was trodden firm by animals. He noticed that sick and wounded animals tried to approach the spring. The hunter remained near this warm water for a few days and felt an influx of vigor. When he came home he told others about it, and pilgrimages to the spring by people with different ailments began.

Today, a sanatorium has arisen near the wonderful spring: a large bathing section, some modern residential accommodations, and a complex of cultural and community services.

The center of the Jewish Autonomous Region is the city of Birobidzhan (where the Rivers Bira and Bidzhan meet). Half a century ago, clothing and textile factories appeared there. In the post-war years, Birobidzhan became a center of the machine building industry. The factory "Dalselkhosmash" produces self-propelling caterpillar combines for rice harvesting and silo clearing.

Two newspapers are published in Birobidzhan in Yiddish and Russian; there is a national theater, a museum, a large library, a music school, and a wide range of secondary schools for general and specialized education.

The city is conveniently situated on both banks of the Bira. Its central avenue carries the name of a Jewish writer of the last century, Sholom Aleichem.

Almost at the eastern border of the Jewish Autonomous Region, on the left side of the *Russia* express as it moves east, passengers can see, on top of a steep volcano mound, a memorial constructed of white stone—a huge figure of a Soviet soldier charging with a rifle. The mound is called Iyun-Koran and the monument commemorates a Civil War battle on this site in 1922. Near the memorial are mass graves of the fallen Red Guards and a museum of the Civil War.

# Khabarovsk: City of Half a Million

The eastern border of the Jewish Autonomous Region passes within a few kilometers of a major industrial center, the principal city of the Khabarovsk Territory—

Khabarovsk (8,533 kilometers from Moscow). The last houses of the Jewish settlement sweep by and the train rolls onto a long railroad bridge across the Amur River. At first, swampy bank, weeds, and sedge appear and then, at last, heavy like mercury, the glistening water of the biggest river of the Far East.

The Amur originates at the confluence of two mountain streams, the Shilka and the Argun, and cuts its way through the tree-covered rocks of the Khingan mountain range.

After leaving the mountains the Amur continues just as stormy and unruly. It divides into several arms, which flow separately or together intermittently, bubbling in a narrow current through a stony pass, or spreading out widely on plains.

Near the city of Blagoveshchensk the Amur receives a tributary from the left: the major river, Zeya. The Amur widens greatly; the average distance between the banks reaches one and a half kilometers. Then the Amur enters the Malyy Khingan Mountains and narrows considerably. The river flows for a long distance between narrow mountain passes, flanked by wild precipitous rocks, and again it pours out in a powerful stream into the valley. Near the city of Khabarovsk, its width is almost three kilometers.

Khabarovsk celebrated its centenary in 1958. The foundations for the first buildings of the future city were laid in the spring of 1848 by a squad of soldiers of the 13th East Siberian battalion. The commander of the battalion, Captain E. M. Dyachenko, gave the settlement, founded by him, the name of Yerofey Pavlovich Khabarov, a Russian traveler.

*V. Kuranov*

The eminent Russian geographer M. I. Venyukov (1832-1901) wrote about the settlement: "It is inevitable that a large city will originate here in the future." Khabarovsk overtook some ancient cities of European Russia in size of population even during the first decades of its existence. The development of the city was particularly rapid after it was connected by railroad with Vladivostok.

Khabarovsk expanded first as an industrial center. Its basic population consisted of workers who, at the beginning of the twentieth century, actively joined the struggle for their rights; they took part in the first Russian revolution of 1905-1907 and in 1917 proclaimed the power of the Soviets as soon as the Socialist Revolution had taken place in Petrograd.

Today 524,000 people live in Khabarovsk, and it remains a city of workers. There are more than a hundred industrial enterprises here, producing diesel engines, lathes, electro-energetic equipment, cables, and much else.

Let us take a walk through Khabarovsk. From the square at the station, streets run south to the bank of the Amur. The main avenues of the city run on three parallel "ridges." Between these heights, stretching from north to south, there used to be ravines, overgrown with shrubs and impassable in rain. Now they are filled in and built over, and the ground is clothed in asphalt.

The principal streets of Khabarovsk are very wide, and the strain of city traffic will not be felt here for a long time. Let us proceed along the centrally located Karl Marx Avenue to the quay. The avenue ends at Komsomol Square, in a park which descends steeply down to the river, a favorite spot for walks. In the summer, orchestras play here; two theatres and a sports complex are nearby.

The steep slopes covered with trees abruptly give way to a wide beach. On weekends, in fine weather, it is usually filled with thousands of relaxing people. River "trams" carry many to the left bank of the Amur where there are endless beaches and still waters, and where an amateur can cast a line and experience the joy of the fisherman.

A very interesting regional museum has been opened in the park, which tells about the history of the peoples of the Far East, the region's present life, and its natural wealth. The museum has many unique exhibits, which always attract the attention of both Soviet and foreign visitors.

Khabarovsk's populace is "younger" than that of many cities of Central Russia, possibly because there is a large student population here. It is not possible to enumerate all the institutes—medical, pedagogic, polytechnic, railroad, physical culture, national economy— in which approximately 40,000 young men and women study.

The Combined Scientific Research Institute of the Academy of Sciences, the Far Eastern Scientific Research Institute of Forestry, with its extensive dendrarium, and the Far Eastern Scientific Research Institute of Agriculture work on problems of economy, sociology, and preservation of the natural environment.

A large group of writers and poets live in Khabarovsk and publish their own thick literary monthly journal, *The Far East.*

*V. Kuranov*

A mass of foreign tourists visit Khabarovsk every year. Most are in transit, traveling to or from Japan. Visitors usually fly from Moscow (eight hours without intermediate stops), stay for a short time in Khabarovsk, and then proceed by comfortable train to Nakhodka to board a ship sailing for Yokohama. Foreign visitors arriving in Khabarovsk on the *Russia* generally do the same.

# Part VIII
# Photographs

Settlement of construction workers ("Svetlyy") engaged in building a hydroelectric power station on the River Zeya. Photograph by V. Marikovsky.

Khabarovsk Territory. Banks of the
Amur. Photograph by U. Muravin.

Khabarovsk. Control desk of oil refinery. Photograph by L. Reznikov.

Khabarovsk. Institute of Physical Culture. Photograph by L. Reznikov.

# Part IX
# The Final Thousand
# Kilometers

## The Nanaytsy

Near Khabarovsk at Lake Petropavlovskoye lies the village of Sikachi-Alyan. Ancient stones with outlines of people, animals, and fish were discovered near this village when the water was low. The academician A.P. Okladnikov, a great expert on Siberia and the Far East, thought that the stone carvings were carved by ancient inhabitants of the Priamurye, the forebears of the Nanaytsy.

Today the Nanaytsy live in the villages of the Khabarovsk Territory north of the Trans-Siberian Line. There are relatively few of them—about 10,000. They prefer to settle along banks of rivers, which serve them as transport arteries: in winter they travel on the ice by reindeer team and in summer by boat.

The Nanaytsy mainly fish and collect ginseng roots. Today they are organized in fishing and hunting cooperatives. The State buys up skins and fish at prices determined by agreement with the kolkhoz and supplies the Nanaytsy with motor boats, rifles, and ammunition. In other words, the basis of the activity of the local kolkhoz is, in principle, the same as in all the other agricultural cooperatives in the country.

The way of life of the Nanaytsy has changed radically during the Soviet era. Poverty, injustice, universal illiteracy, and ignorance have forever receded into the past. The elements of Soviet civilization consolidate themselves ever more broadly and firmly in the life and conditions of the Nanaytsy, who have acquired full rights and have become active builders of the new life. Among their youth there is 100 percent literacy, their intelligentsia grows in numbers, and there is an intellectual upsurge of the people as a whole. The Nanaytsy are doctors, engineers, zoologists, forest cultivators, etc. From among their numbers have come eminent scientists, writers, and people active in the field of culture. The prose writer Grigory Khodzher is well known to lovers of contemporary Soviet literature; his books have been translated into the many languages of the U.S.S.R. It is hard to believe that such an intellectual leap occurred in one generation. A characteristic example is that of the old hunter Polokto Kile, who can neither read nor write, who does not know in what year he was born nor how old he is. But all his sons and daughters went to school, and two of them received a university education.

All of them work. Note their occupations: director of the teaching department of a secondary school, mathematics teacher, party activist, movie operator, and motor mechanic. Little from the previous life style remains in the spacious Kile home. In the rooms there is modern furniture, a radio receiver, a television set, and various domestic appliances.

The reader could object by pointing out that this is only one example, which need not necessarily represent the true situation. There cannot be any disagreement with such an argument. However, here are some general data. In the Far East, there are 23 persons with advanced education for every thousand inhabitants; the average is 22 for the whole of the country. For every 10,000 inhabitants of the Far East, there are 160 students in institutions of higher education. Decide for yourself if these are many or few. For purposes of comparison, it must be noted that in both the German Federal Republic and in England, there are only 40-50 students per 10,000 inhabitants.

It is especially interesting to be in a Nanaytsy village on the day of a festival. In the past, the Nanaytsy had, of course, their various festivals and rituals, but one way or another, these were tied up with their religion— shamanism. The shaman was not merely a servant of the cult; he gave orders and exercised power in the whole district. To disobey the shaman meant to be cursed by him and to attract a host of "evil spirits." For centuries, ignorant people bowed down before everything the shaman said or did. Remember the story about the teacher Arkadi Loskutov, who came to the Mansi in the 1920's? The same situation also applied to the Nanaytsy, the same cruel and irreconcilable struggle between light and darkness, reason and ignorance. The eternal passion of people for knowledge and discovery won. The first discovery for the Nanaytsy, as well as for the Khanty, was this:

one need not listen to what the shaman says, one need not do what he orders, and generally one can live without him. With difficulty and pain came the break in consciousness, and the turning away from prejudice and superstition to knowledge, to conscious labor, and to a new life.

It isn't possible to read without agitation an extract from the minutes of the first convention of representatives of local ethnic groups from the Khabarovsk Territory in 1921. This is where the Nanaytsy, the Orochi, and other indigenous ethnic groups of this region started on the road to Socialism. "1. Having considered the question from all sides, it was found that the existing alien custom—the marriage of minors, that is, two-year-olds with minors, or children (girls) of five and six years with men of 20 to 30 years, [and] the purchase and sale of brides—is superseded. We consider such marriage immoral and absolutely harmful for the descendants. 2. The old custom of marriage is to be abolished and to be considered completely impermissible, and we are to be guided completely in this prohibition by the Workers' and Peasants' Government, namely: a bride younger than 16 years cannot be given away and a man cannot be married under the age of 18 years. The marriage must be entered into without any constraint from any side and with the mutual agreement of the groom and bride. 3. The old custom of sending a woman in labor into a cold tent in winter is to be abolished, and we are to adhere strictly to the rules regarding childbirth which modern medicine requires. . ."

A Nanaytsy festival day is a colorful and impressive spectacle. Many wear their traditional national costumes, cloth gowns of ancient cut, embellished with embroidery and appliqued with colored fabrics. There is a brightness and harmony of colors. On the feet are boots sewn from deer hide or slippers with a beautiful ornament. Many young men and women wear modern clothes and carry portable tape recorders and transistors.

No festival can do without exciting competitions, and since these are usually held in winter, there are races with reindeer teams and on skis. There are songs by the local amateur choir. And one more typical feature must be noted—the isolation and seclusion common among separate ethnic groups has disappeared. At the festival of the Nanaytsy can be seen faces of Russians and Ukrainians who live in the same village with the Nanaytsy or in neighboring villages.

## Komsomolsk-on-the-Amur: Symbol of Courage and Labor

Before reaching Khabarovsk, the train passes the small, undistinguished station of Dezhnevka, from which a line branches off to Komsomolsk-on-the-Amur, the second largest city of the Khabarovsk Territory. The Baykal-Amur Line cuts its way to Khabarovsk-on-the-Amur from Lena (which is east of Bratsk) through mountains and swamps, taiga and permafrost. But the "construction of the century" is also being undertaken west of the Amur. First a bridge over the Amur was built in 1976 to connect the B.A.M. with the already operating railroad to Sovetskaya Gavan.

Emigrants from the Perm Region (we passed through it during the first day of our journey) settled on the site of what would later be Komsomolsk-on-the-Amur. The new village was named Permskoye, and it was visited several years later by some geographers who wrote in their report to the governor: "Although this appears to be a locality convenient for settlement, it does not forecast a good future, either by its area or by the quality of the land and situation in comparison with other localities, since this locale is low lying and distant from mountain slopes. . ." And this is how it was until the Soviet government began to carry into practice bold plans of industrializing thinly populated districts.

A resolution was adopted in the Kremlin on February 23, 1932, to lay the foundations for a city in the district of the village, and to develop heavy industry there. The first detachment of construction workers arrived in Permskoye from Khabarovsk on the steamships *Komintern* and *Kolumb*. The young pioneers had been directed there by the organization of Communist Youth (Komsomol) from many cities of the country. The Komsomoltsy decided to erect the new city in the Far East with their own hands, as an industrial base and bridgehead, from which a powerful advance of Soviet civilization into the huge, thinly peopled region could be undertaken. The settlers knew that unbelievably hard work and exceptionally difficult living conditions were to be expected, but they were prepared. Patriotism and youthful eagerness turned out to be stronger than the harshness of nature and the discomfort of the living conditions. At first the construction workers lived in tents; they even spent the winter in them. Gradually they moved into new timber houses which smelled of resin.

Within two months and 10 days of the disembarkation of the first detachment, a whistle sounded over the Amur, announcing the launching of a saw mill, the first industrial undertaking of the future city. Soon the village was renamed: the city of Komsomolsk-on-the-Amur.

One winter a hitch occurred in the supply of timber to the sawmill. The young men and women grabbed picks, crowbars, and spades and cut a channel nine kilometers long into the ice of the river so that the logs could float from the place where they had been cut. Day and night, in a fierce frost, they pushed the logs along the water with boathooks. The splashes of water immediately froze on their clothing. After a few hours, the workers were stiff, almost blocks of ice. A special Komsomol brigade drove away the half-frozen people, for thawing out and a change of clothing; then they returned to the "icy track."

In 1942, the "Amurstal" works produced the first lot of metal. The veterans of the construction of these works remember: "Among us there were even pastry cooks. The boys joked: this, they said, is a related profession, it is also necessary to work near a furnace." Hundreds of heavy industrial plants were under construction in the country, cadres of workers were required everywhere, and yesterday's carpenters took a position at cupola furnaces, and hairdressers and lumberjacks mastered the refinements of operating open-hearth furnaces.

Nearly 40 years have elapsed since then. Komsomolsk has become a huge industrial center. Ships come down from the slipways, the most complicated lathes are dispatched to all corners of the country, and a new industry has developed— oil refining.

Once there were only 51 families in Permskoye. Today more than a quarter of a million people live in the city, which continues to grow rapidly: new industrial enterprises begin operations, the scope of community services expands, and construction workers for the B.A.M. keep on arriving.

How many books, films, and plays about the enthusiasm for work and the self-sacrifice of the first builders of this city have been made in the Soviet Union! Komsomolsk has become a symbol of the new attitude toward life and its purpose; it has become a beacon for generations of youth.

And if in our days young lads and girls go to work on Siberian construction sites, in their urge to assert themselves, to try their strength, and to check their ability to bear hardships, then somewhere deep in their souls this impulse has been prompted by the Komsomoltsy of the 1930's.

In the spring of 1978, Leonid Brezhnev completed his journey on the Trans-Siberian Line at Komsomolsk-on-the-Amur. Addressing himself to the representative of the workers of the city, he said that the majestic panorama of the city built on a site where, not long ago, there was dense taiga, left an immense impression. For all the inhabitants of Komsomolsk-on-the-Amur, he wished that the city remain youthful, multiply its glorious traditions, and constitute, for all present and future generations, a symbol of courage, labor, and heroism.

Those who come to the city today can observe the touching solicitude with which the present generation carefully preserves everything connected with the exploit of the pioneers. A granite monolith has been erected on what is a historical spot, with the words carved upon it: "Here the first Komsomoltsy-builders of the city disembarked on May 10, 1932." Nearby is a youth center. In the local museum the silent witnesses to the feat have been collected: diaries, primitive instruments, photographs of those who today are respectfully called veterans. Many of them still live here. Of course, they are pleased that they are known and remembered, and that they serve as an example. They look with unconcealed pride at contemporary Komsomolsk and on those immense achievements in Siberia which they started with their own hands. They were the first.

In the distant 1930's the young people had already learned how to build so as not to ruin the forest needlessly, how to take care of the environment, and how to preserve nature in its original state, where possible. Adjoining the city are 30,000 hectares of virgin taiga— the Komsomolskiy Sanctuary. As in every sanctuary, rare kinds of animals and plants are protected. At the same time, its active purpose is to demonstrate visibly to today's new arrivals in Siberia that man's creative activity should improve nature.

If you travel by train from Komsomolsk-on-the-Amur to Sovetskaya Gavan, traveling companions who are old residents of this area will tell you, without fail, about the Tumninskiye hot springs, not far from the pass across the Sikhote-Alin mountain range. It is said that the springs are distinguished by their really miraculous healing qualities. Many travelers gather there to test their effect on themselves. Unfortunately, difficulties in access have made it impossible so far to build a resort on the site.

The whole Sikhote-Alin coastline has been declared a sanctuary zone: the law prohibits the industrial exploitation of the forest. It has been proposed to preserve the green border of the sea forever. Only in the depth of the taiga are minor logging operations and limited hunting of fur animals permitted.

The principal inhabited places of this district are concentrated at the foot of the Sikhote-Alin Mountains. The population of the coastal villages has increased to 66,000 people, compared with 280 in 1926. These villages are spread around Sovetskaya Gavan, a spacious city well-provided with up-to-date facilities and a large and well-equipped cultural center. Nearby is the port of Vanino from which cargo in transit is dispatched to overseas countries and to Chukotka, Kamchatka, and Sakhalin. A rail ferry circulates between Vanino and the Sakhalin port of Kholmsk. In the not too distant future, Sovetskaya Gavan and Vanino will play an important part in the cargo transport of the Baykal-Amur Line.

After Khabarovsk, the Trans-Siberian Line turns fairly sharply south from the east-west direction and runs along the Ussuri River, beyond which lies the territory of the Chinese People's Republic. At times the railroad passes within about five kilometers from the border.

At some 70 kilometers from Khabarovsk the line crosses the small River Khor. This is the southern boundary of the Bolshe-Khekhzirskiy Sancturary, which occupies an area of 46,000 hectares. One of the small ethnic groups of the Far East, the Udegeytsy, has a legend about this locale:

"Two birds, flying toward each other, collided in the white fog and dropped their load. They had been sent by the good spirit of the South and the good spirit of the North to throw seeds on the desert plains and mountains. Since then, wild grapes wind around pine trees, and the northern berry *klukva* grows side by side with the aralia— a Far Eastern spiky palm with meter-long leaves."

Khekhzirskiy vegetation is strictly limited by the altitude of its location. The foot of the mountains, where our train passes, is covered with leafy species. On the slopes, the trees which predominate are varieties of cedar, ash, "Amur-velvet," with a blackish-dove color bark from which cork is obtained, and Manchurian nut trees. On the higher parts of the mountains grow angular pines and fir trees. And all this is tied up with lianas and other winding plants. In the Bolshe-Khekhzirskiy Sanctuary there are noble roedeer, brown and Himalayan bears, lynx and sables.

There is immense pleasure in watching the spring flight of the water birds. Imagine a sunset when all nature falls silent, as it were, in expectation of sleep. And suddenly, from the south, in the light of the dying rays, thousands of ducks return in a flock to their native places. They come down on the small lake, filling the air with the sound of their flapping wings. Scarcely visible through the live black cover, the sky appears here and there as flashes of pink. Dark dots drop onto the water and vanish in it. And again there is such silence, that the watcher involuntarily wonders whether he had not actually dreamed the winged cloud.

The Far East is rich in sanctuaries, so many, it isn't possible to mention all of them. But man, who creates them, has one design for all the sanctuaries: to preserve nature in an untouched condition, to enable people to know the natural environment. And who knows, the sanctuaries in these parts may one day be places of pilgrimage for naturalists from all over the world, for here there will be a visible example of the unity and interaction of nature and man.

# The Maritime Territory: Unique Nature

Two hundred kilometers beyond Khabarovsk a bridge spans the River Bikin and our train crosses into the Maritime Territory.

About 80 percent of the territory is taken up by mountains. Their characteristic peculiarity is their low height and softness, and their roundness of shape. Sopki, stony, conical, volcanic hills overgrown with forest, glide past the coach windows.

The climate of the Maritime Territory is governed by winds. In winter, the wind blows from the land to the sea, bringing with it severe frosts. In summer, the wind blows only from the ocean, the air becomes saturated with moisture, and there are frequent rains and sometimes heavy downpours. The rains and the abundant summer sunshine contribute to a lush vegetation in the Maritime Territory. The phenomenon of giant plants occurs here. Grass reaches the level of human height, and an adult man can hide under an ordinary burdock.

More than 200 species of trees and shrubs grow in the Maritime Territory, and up to 2,000 species of grass, some of which are found nowhere else: the "basket" willow, the "shrub" birch and the "iron" birch, and a special species of bird-cherry tree. The plant referred to as *neogen* goes back to the beginning of the Quaternary period. Ginseng, the "root of life," is also found in the Maritime Territory in a wild form, although it is also cultivated on special plantations.

The hunter can come across the trail of a handsome tiger. A rare species of tortoise and several other animals dwell only here. The spotted stag, an inhabitant of the forests, is valued for his set of young antlers, which are used in the preparation of valuable medicines.

Tin and polymetallic ores are mined, but only lead and silver are processed locally. Ores of other metals are dispatched for processing to various cities of the country, since the energy base of the region is comparatively undeveloped, as is the production of chemical ingredients used in refining metals. The problems of chemical raw material and electric power are being resolved at an increasing rate. Coal deposits have already been discovered, and thermoelectric stations are being built to provide cheap local fuel. Geologists hypothesize that the whole of the lowlands of the Amur delta represents one huge coal basin.

The volcanic hills recede further and further. The Trans-Siberian Line runs along the Ussuri Lowlands. Swampy areas overgrown with reeds come into view, and so do fields of soya, potatoes, and other vegetables.

And there comes the River Iman. The Iman basin is the main gold producing district of the Maritime Territory. The largest gold fields—Nezametnyy[46] and Blagodatnyy[47]—are located along the central section of the

[46] Invisible.
[47] Beneficial.

river and at its source. Non-ferrous metals are also mined on the Iman.

The river is not large: nevertheless, during summer rains it overflows its banks, carries away bridges, and floods bordering settlements. More than once, its waters have stopped traffic on the railroad. Now the flow of water is regulated by a hydrotechnic installation.

In the center section of the Iman basin lies Kartun, the oldest settlement of gold prospectors and hunters. In the administration building of the gold fields, a very interesting collection has been assembled: there are gold nuggets of 100-150 grams, samples of gold-bearing sand, and gold quartz conglomerates.

The Kartun game and forestry base is engaged in catching tigers, wild cats, roebucks, striped squirrels, goats, tortoises, and snakes for zoos. It also handles different nuts, berries, mushrooms, and medicinal herbs, among them, ginseng.

Having passed the town of Iman, the *Russia* express arrives at Lesozavodsk. Beyond Lesozavodsk, 30-50 kilometers west of the railroad, is Lake Khanka, 4,000 square kilometers in area and up to four meters deep. It is not famous for its size, but rather for the rarest species of plants: the lotus flower, the *eurea* with its giant "jugs" and leaves two meters wide, and the water nut. East of the lake are lowlands where spring wheat, oats, and soya are grown as well as rice. The local State farm uses machinery extensively for preparing and working over the rice paddies, rectangular lots divided by earth banks. Aircraft sow the rice as well as fertilize the fields. Thus organized, rice growing yields big harvests, brings in a large income, and saves labor considerably.

The economic center of the district is the town of Spassk-Dalniy (with about 52,000 inhabitants). It has enterprises for the repair of agricultural machinery, a meat works, a vegetable- and fruit-preserving factory, and other industrial facilities. The production of the local cement works is based on the limestone and clay obtained on the outskirts of the town.

In the square in front of the railroad station, a monument has been erected to commemorate the Red Guards killed in a battle which took place at the approaches to Spassk-Dalniy in 1922, the last year of the Civil War.

## Ussuriysk: Ginseng Plantations

The great Siberian Line continues further and further toward the southwest. The train stops at a big station: the city of Ussuriysk has a population of 147,000. Situated in the center of a fertile valley, its economy is mainly oriented toward the processing of agricultural raw materials. The largest enterprises are the Zhirkombinat"[48] and the sugar factory. A machine factory produces woodworking lathes, equipment for the forest industry, washing machines, and refrigerators; there is also a factory producing building materials and one that makes furniture. In the city there are three theatres, a pedagogic and agricultural institute, two special secondary schools, and a network of schools for general education.

Ussuriysk has a clearly defined street plan. Along its streets, plantings consist of trees and shrubs transplanted

[48] Combined fat works.

from the taiga: poplars, elms, jasmine, among many. The city park leaves a pleasant impression, as does the fruit tree plantations in the suburbs.

Fifty kilometers east of Ussuriysk, a sanctuary extends over the slopes of the mountain ridge at the source of the River Suputinka. It was founded in 1932 by a botanist and geographer, the academician V. L. Komarov (1869-1945), and within the sanctuary is the late scientist's summer house. It was constructed from all kinds of timber growing in these parts. The sanctuary takes up 17,000 hectares. More than 800 species of plants of the highest order and about 200 species of edible mushrooms are protected in it. But the pride of the sanctuary is the medicinal and rare aralia plant. All the species of this family known to science are here.

Ginseng, which belongs to the aralia family, grows wild in the sanctuary, but it is also cultivated on a special plantation. There, the seeds of the ginseng germinate in the first year, while under natural conditions the seeds germinate in the second year.

The Mountain-Taiga Far Eastern Nature Station is situated along the middle section of the Suputinka River. Experiments here are concerned with acclimatizing southern plants to the Far East and developing new strains of grapes and spreading, low-growing plants.

The journey on the Suiyfun and Suputinka Rivers must give great pleasure to a skilled canoeist who is not afraid of difficulties and who can paddle against the current or tow the canoe where necessary. He can see wonderful landscapes and picturesque mountain gorges, and become acquainted with the varied and rich Far Eastern vegetation. It is not for nothing that scientists have favored this district for nature studies.

Twenty-two kilometers from the city of Ussuriysk is the rail junction of Baranovskiy.

Experimental vineyards are located in Gvosdevo some 180 kilometers west of Baranovskiy. More than 60 varieties of grapes developed in the Far East are subjected to tests here. Among them, the "Khassanskiy Boussa" and the "Khassanskiy Sweet" have a prodigious growth (up to 130 hundredweights per hectare), and can also withstand relatively strong frosts (up to 30-35° below zero) without harm.

# Nakhodka—An International Tourist Port

From Ugolnaya Station, the Trans-Siberian Line runs in two directions: south to Vladivostok and east to the port of Nakhodka.

Before proceeding further to Vladivostok, let us visit the places along the eastern branch of the line.

The first major station is called Uglovaya.[49] The city to which it provides access carries the name of a Russian revolutionary, the Bolshevik Artem [the underground *nom-de-guerre* of Fyodor Sergeyev (1883-1921)]. The city has a population of 70,000 and sits atop the center of a coal basin. A thermoelectric power station has been built here, using local brown coal and providing power for the whole of the Maritime Territory. The miners' settlements of Artem are spread widely over the basin. Mines alternate with enterprises of the building industry.

[49] Literally, "on the corner."

V. *Kuranov*

Light industry is also represented in Artem: one factory produces carpets, another pianos, and there is an experimental porcelain factory.

The train travels along the vally of the Suchan River. Here comes a minor station called Maykhe where a large State farm breeds spotted deer.

And again a major mining town—Suchan—which, like Artem, brings into its orbit many miners' settlements and thus extends for 30 kilometers over volcanic mounds and valleys.

Different kinds of coal are mined in Suchan, among which semi-anthracite is exported to Japan. The sorting of coal takes place on the spot in a large enrichment plant.

Suchan also abounds in gardens and vineyards. The climate here is mild, and the abundant humidity makes it possible to grow grapes the tastiness of which compares favorably with the celebrated southern grapes.

Losovaya, with a nearby major thermoelectric power plant, is the next station. It supplies power for the mining districts of the Sikhote-Alin. The place is famous for its healthy climate and an abundance of interesting natural nooks. A tourist base, Mountain Springs, has been established here.

And at last Nakhodka, a major harbor city with a population of 129,000 people.

The city extends for 30 kilometers over the mountainous coastline of the ice-free bay of Nakhodka. One of the youngest cities of the Maritime Territory, it celebrated its 25th jubilee comparatively recently.

International cargo and passenger lines connect Nakhodka with the ports of Japan, India, Thailand,

Singapore, and Hong Kong. The passenger line Nakhodka-Yokohama is serviced by first class Soviet ocean liners which carry thousands of tourists every year.

Metal-cutting lathes, cut timber, coal, chemical raw materials, cast iron, ores, etc., are exported to Japan through Nakhodka. Coastal trade between Soviet ports and Japanese cities on the western coast of the island of Honshu is also being developed. Soviet cities supply their Japanese partners with shark fins, the roe of sea urchins, and dried trepang, as well as usable waste from wood processing.

Nakhodka serves as a base for active deep sea fishing. A seafaring college of the fishing industry trains the personnel in command of fishing trawlers, floating bases, and factories. There are also two seafaring schools which give their graduates a special secondary education.

The principal avenue of Nakhodka, Nakhodkinskiy Prospect, runs over the volcanic mounds along the coastline of the bay, somewhat above the wharves and harbor structures, and unites the city into a whole. Architects have located a sports stadium where the volcanic mounds recede somewhat from the coastline. The city park has been laid out around the small Solionnyy Lake.

The "second stage" of Nakhodka, Port Vostochnyy,[50] has been under construction for several years on the other side of the bay. Through Vostochnyy will pass the ever-increasing stream of goods to the districts of the Soviet Far North. An important role in the development of mutually advantageous trade and economic links

[50] Eastern.

between the U.S.S.R. and Asian countries, Oceania and America, has been allotted to the new port. Japanese firms are taking part in the building of Vostochnyy by supplying harbor equipment on credit.

The shipment of cargoes, dispatched from Tokyo, Sydney, Hong Kong, and Los Angeles, through Nakhodka, and further by the Trans-Siberian Line, to the cities of Western Europe proved to be much cheaper than the delivery by the traditional sea route. The route through Nakhodka is 14 times shorter than that from the Pacific Ocean to the Atlantic around Africa, and seven times shorter than the route through the Panama Canal.

Ships having a loading capacity of up to 150,000 tons will be able to berth at the coal storage wharves of Vostochnyy. In an hour, the machinery installed here can load 8,000 tons of coal delivered to the port from southern Yakutiya by the B.A.M.

The manager of port construction at Vostochnyy, Valentin Petkov, says: "Port Vostochnyy will have four wharves which will stretch along the bay for 14 kilometers. Eight specialized cargo areas have been designed. Mechanization of all work has been provided for. Programmed control and a radar system will make it possible to determine the course into the Bay of Vostochnyy of vessels already at the approach to Nakhodka Bay."

But Vostochnyy will be most directly concerned with the B.A.M. which is under construction. In the first place, in the opinion of economists, Vostochnyy will take over the handling of the "big coal" of the B.A.M., as the main port in the eastern part of the country and the one from which coal ships laden with Yakutiyan coal for northern Soviet towns and other countries will depart. Here the transport routes from the Pacific Ocean through Siberia to Europe will begin. Business people call this "export of transit services," and while the Trans-Siberian Line presently takes part in it, its capacity in this respect is limited. When the B.A.M. reaches the Pacific, the "export of transit services" will increase considerably, and international transport by container ships will begin on a large scale. Sovetskaya Gavan, Vanino, Nakhodka, and Vostochnyy will become the starting and destination ports for the intercontinental through-transport of goods. The B.A.M. and the eastern ports of the U.S.S.R. will link Europe with the Pacific Ocean with firm ties of business cooperation.

# Part IX
## Photographs

Leonid Brezhnev among the young
builders of the Baykal-Amur Railroad.
Photograph by B. Musaelian.

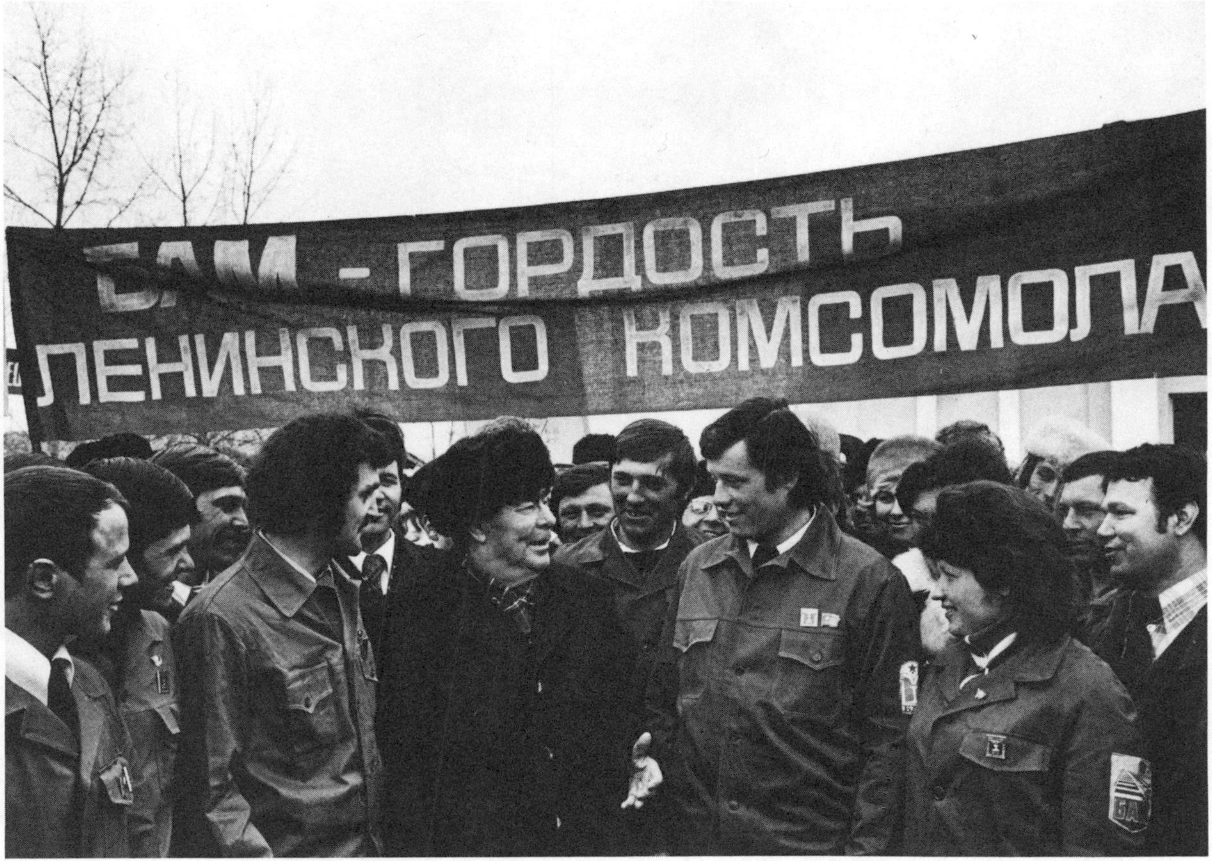
БАМ - ГОРДОСТЬ
ЛЕНИНСКОГО КОМСОМОЛА

Komsomolsk-on-the-Amur. "House of Youth" swimming pool. Photograph by U. Muravin.

Sikhote-Alin Sanctuary. Spotted stag.
Photograph by V. Kasho.

Sikhote-Alin Sanctuary. White mushroom. Photograph by V. Kasho.

Tiger in snow. Ussuriysk District. Photograph by D. Debabov.

Maritime Territory. Sanatorium "Okeansky." Photograph by U. Muravin.

Vladivostok Harbor at night. Photograph by U. Muravin.

# Part X
# The End of the Journey

## Vladivostok: 9,300 kilometers from Moscow

From Ugolnaya Station, the Trans-Siberian Line turns south and enters the peninsula named in honor of the famous Russian navigator Nikolai Mouraviov-Amursky (1809-1881). The peninsula is washed by the waters of the Bay of Peter the Great. The highest volcanic mound of the peninsula—the Eagle's Nest—rises 214 meters above sea level. A 180-meter high filigree television tower, the first visible feature of the city, has been erected upon it.

At first the train passes the resort suburbs of Vladivostok: Sad-Gorod,[51] Okeanskaya, and Sedanka. A mild climate, forest-covered mounds, convenient beaches, healing mud baths, and a high concentration of salts in the sea water attract seekers of relaxation from the whole

[51] Garden City.

of the Far East, Siberia, and even European Russia. Sanatoria and rest homes stretch in a continuous band along the railroad. Botanical gardens, in which practically all species of plants indigenous to the southern maritime taiga have been planted, have also been laid out here.

Then the city proper starts. Terraced and steeply inclined streets stretch along the slopes of the volcanic mounds descending to the sea. Some streets end abruptly, others extend over long distances. Ancient buildings combine with new multistory ones, high-rise towers share the streets with more horizontal developments.

The bays, which cut deeply into the coastline, and the rows of mounds divide the city into separate "townships" connected by trains and ferries, buses, trolley buses, electric trains, and even a funicular railway.

The main part of the city is situated around the Zolotoy Rog[52] Cove, which penetrates deeply into the peninsula.

Vladivostok's major street, named after Lenin, stretches along the cove for seven kilometers. A broad set of steps leads to the edge of the water. The yacht club, Dynamo Stadium, and a sandy beach are located there.

On Lenin Street is the Drama Theatre, the Theatre of the Young Spectator, movies, the Far Eastern Polytechnic Institute, the Institute of Fishing Industry, hotels, and the Palace of Culture.

Descending from one side of Lenin Street are gardens which alternate with residential blocks and terraced overlooks from which there is a good view of the city. In one of the garden squares a memorial sculpture has been

[52] Golden Horn.

erected for Sergei Lazo, a hero of the Civil War. On the overlooks, memorials have also been erected to Admiral G. I. Nevelskiy (1813-1876) and to the sailors of the merchant navy who perished in the Second World War.

Lenin Street intersects Okeanskiy Prospect[53] at the central square of the city. There, a momument commemorates the fighters for the Soviets in the Far East during the Civil War. The wharves and stores of the commercial and fishing port, and the docks and workshops of the ship repair works, form an uninterrupted band many kilometers long along the southern and southeastern coastline of the Zolotoy Rog Cove. Huge cranes rumble and tugboats and fishing trawlers continually furrow the water.

Vladivostok is a major industrial center among whose more important industrial enterprises are: the "Radiopribor" works, a factory producing mining equipment, factories producing prefabricated components for residential construction, meat works and flour mills, fish processing works, a factory producing confectionery, a furniture factory, and the Vladivostok pharmaceutical works producing medicines and healing preparations made from local plants, sea kale, ginseng root, and the antlers of the spotted deer.

In 1960, Vladivostok celebrated its centenary. The history of the city began with the disembarkation in the cove of a group of sailors and soldiers who had been assigned to find a site for a naval defense strongpoint. A monument has been erected in the city to the memory of this event: a column crowned with the model of the sailing ship *Manchur*, which brought the group into the

[53] Ocean Avenue.

cove. At the base of the column stand the figures of a sailor and a soldier. On the column a vertical inscription in cast letters spells out "Vladivostok," and below, a marble tablet repeats the words of V. I. Lenin: "Vladivostok is far away, but it is our city."

Vladivostok, with a population numbering 536,000, continues to develop. In 1971-1975 almost 1,000 million roubles were invested in construction work throughout the city. New blocks of well-equipped residential buildings have been erected in many districts. Vladivostok has moved far to the east, toward the Ussuriysk Bay, and climbed upward along the slopes of the Eagle's Nest, in in the center. At the same time, the Drama Theatre, the State Circus, the Railroad Post Office, the Hotel Vladivostok, a community services center, a department store, and several other important buildings were erected.

Even broader perspectives open up before the city in the current five-year period (1976-1980). The main attention is directed toward the building of housing, schools, hospitals, cultural facilities, and community services. Only 9-, 12-, and 16-story buildings will be erected. Construction of five-story buildings will be completely discontinued. All that has been built to date will become a characteristic background to the new Vladivostok. The skyline of the city will change visibly. The basic intent of further development of this largest Soviet city at the Pacific Ocean is that it be modern, architecturally purposeful, and provide the best facilities.

In recent years, Vladivostok has been mentioned more frequently in the pages of the world press. In November, 1974, the Soviet-American summit meeting took place there. It led to an understanding between the

U.S.S.R. and the U.S.A. concerning the conclusion of a long-term agreement on the limitation of strategic arms. In April, 1978, Leonid Brezhnev, addressing the participants of the school of the Red Banner Pacific Ocean Fleet, gave an exhausting analysis of talks with the United States on this question. Brezhnev emphasized that the Soviet Union will continue its efforts to achieve a steadfast progress toward military defusing and transition to real disarmament.

Vladivostok has appeared in the world arena before. Several major scientific research institutes studying the world's oceans and its inhabitants are in Vladivostok. Its scientists are frequent participants in many international symposia on problems of fish reserves and the protection of the natural environment. On the whole, Vladivostok is the largest scientific center in the Soviet Far East. Nine institutions of higher education and 14 technical schools train specialists in diverse fields for the whole Maritime Territory.

From one of the overlooks of the city one can see some of the islands of the Russian Archipelago in the Bay of Peter the Great. Most of these islands serve as places to which tourists come to rest and walk. On the islands of Rimsky-Korsakov a reserve has been created where spotted deer dwell.

On the eastern side of the Bay of Peter the Great is Putyatin Island. It has wooded parks and Goussinoye Lake, where the inhabitants of Vladivostok come to admire the flowering lotus.

Only a few kilometers of the journey are left. The train approaches Vladivostok Station.

From the windows of the train, the Zolotoy Rog

Cove becomes visible, surrounded by a multitude of wharves and ships and a forest of cranes. The cove and the multistory buildings bordering it give the city a unique appearance. The cove is beautiful seen through the breaks in the milky cover of mist or through a curtain of drizzling rain, as well as on a sunny day. And at night, the dark, smooth water flashes and twinkles with the reflections of thousands of lights of different colors.

*     *     *

Our long journey on the Trans-Siberian Line has come to an end. We spent 170 hours and 5 minutes traveling: one week, two hours, and five minutes.

During those seven days you have become acquainted with dozens of cities and towns of Central Russia, the Urals and Siberia, and found out about their history and points of interest. We described the industrial and social aspects of Siberia and of the life of its people, which is full of excitement. We told you of those who went out to conquer that austere land. You have received an impression of the natural environment, of the climatic conditions, and of the wealth beneath the ground of the territories along the line, as well as far beyond it.

Siberia is a storehouse of wealth: oil, natural gas, coal, iron, nickel, lead, tin, chrome, bauxite, alumina, wolfram, asbestos, platinum, silver, and gold. It has been calculated that half the world's reserves of coal, 40 percent of the different minerals, and 33 percent of the world's timber are concentrated in Siberia.

The development of Siberia on an immense scale did not start yesterday. In April, 1918, six months after the victory of the October Revolution, Lenin posed the question of the overall development of the Ural-Kuznetsk District, in the south of Siberia. He drew the attention of the Party to the importance of studying the energy resources of Siberian rivers. The particular significance of Siberia's natural resources for the industrial development of the whole country was emphasized in the first Soviet economic plan GOELRO (Gossudarstvennaya Electrifikaziya Rossii)[54] which was prepared on the initiative of Lenin to cover a timespan of 10 to 15 years. This was in 1920. While the bloody battles of the Civil War were still raging, the Kremlin was already preparing a grandiose economic program. The GOELRO Plan made provision for the construction of a series of major plants for metallurgy and machine building, as well as thermoelectric power stations in Siberia.

The thirties are rightfully considered the beginning of the industrial rise of Siberia. If in the course of the first two Five-Year Plans (1929-1937) the production of the whole of Soviet industry increased five times, in Siberia it increased more than nine times.

In principle, a different direction in the development of Siberia was taken in the post-war period. Instead of the formation of separate industrial centers and cities, there began the creation of industrial complexes comprising huge geographic districts. For example, the Angara-Yenisey industrial complex includes the Irkutsk hydroelectric power station on the Angara (1956), the Novosibirsk H.E.S. on the Ob (1959), the Bratsk H.E.S. on the Angara (1961), as well as dozens of industrial

---

[54] State Electrification Plan of Russia.

enterprises and new cities and towns which grew up in the huge district between Novosibirsk and Irkutsk. Based on cheap electric power, Siberia soon became the center for the production of aluminum for the whole of the Soviet Union. A large chemical industry also came to Siberia in the form of combined cellulose and paper works and oil refining.

The first diamond-bearing Kimberlite shaft was discovered in Yakutiya in 1954. The industrial mining of diamonds began three years later in the shafts "Mir,"[55] "Udachnaya,"[56] and "Aikhal." The first oil well began gushing in the Tyumen district in 1960, and since then, Siberian oil has occupied a first-rank position in Soviet economic plans.

According to the Tenth Five-Year Plan for the development of the national economy of the U.S.S.R. (1976-1980), the development of the West Siberian complex will be continued, with the aim of increasing oil and gas production from the Tyumen resources, where the scale of capital construction is about to be increased two to three times.

In Eastern Siberia, the Sayan complex alone, which will receive its power from the Sayano-Shushenskaya hydroelectric station, the most powerful in the world, will comprise several new major industrial centers for metallurgy and machine building. And, finally, the construction of the Baykal-Amur Railroad, a powerful lever in the economic development of the districts of the Far-East country, will be continued.

In the realization of these programs which are

---

[55] Peace.
[56] The successful one.

grandiose in their scale, a special place belongs to Siberian science. In Novosibirsk, Irkutsk, Tomsk, and Vladivostok geologists and hydrologists, physicists and industrial chemists, economists and sociologists are engaged in bringing the Five-Year Plan to fruition.

Simultaneously with the factories, power stations, coal mines, and oil wells, the whole social infrastructure will be developed, including housing, provision of goods and services, and community facilities. This was clearly stated in the addresses by Leonid Brezhnev during his journey through the districts of Siberia and the Far East. Man, his requirements and conditions of life, his continuous spiritual and moral perfection, are, have always been, and will continue to be central to the policy of the Communist Party. And those great accomplishments which take place in the country and in Siberia, in particular, have been governed by a single principle— the concern for man.

*     *     *

Anyone traveling east by train through Siberia cannot help noticing the dozens of freight trains rushing past in the opposite direction: tanker cars with oil, platform cars with lumber and timber, cars laden with bread and coal and equipment packed in crates. At the railroad junctions stand hundreds of trains loaded with structural components of reinforced concrete and steel, with motor cars, with container crates full of sophisticated apparatus and goods for mass consumption, all consigned for Siberia. A colossal and ever-growing exchange of goods is carried on between the European part of the country and the East.

## V. Kuranov

Along the whole Trans-Siberian Line there is not a single town which has not been surrounded by a whole belt of construction. Blocks of dwellings and buildings for factories and workshops rise everywhere. An objective assessment based on many signs leads to the conclusion that up to and including the Urals, and further, right up to the Pacific Ocean, there reigns a spirit of intense activity and vitality.

Let us hear from the foreign visitors, who, during recent years, have undertaken journeys into different districts of Siberia—they are, in the main, businessmen and journalists who have already seen everything, and not only through the window of the express train. They have been on the Ob, where the oil rigs have become an inalienable part of the landscape; in Mirnyy, where diamonds are mined, and in Bratsk, where, in a giant factory, wood is turnd into cellulose. Finally, they have been on the construction site of the B.A.M., both where construction trains already move and where a tiny clearing has been cut; and they have also been some distance away from the line, where industrial centers are to spring up in future.

Having returned from the eastern districts of the U.S.S.R., the French writer Pierre Gamarra related that he had seen one continuous construction site—Siberia! The American businessman D. Tomb evaluated what he had seen in his own way. The Siberia of today, he said, makes an enormous impression. In the world practice of developing new territories, this is a fantastic phenomenon. Two circumstances are particularly remarkable— the rapid economic progress and the readiness of a great mass of people to go to new districts with difficult natural conditions.

For the Danish journalist Palle Anderson, the B.A.M. was associated with Soviet youth, with its burning patriotism, romantic spirit, and impetuous humor. Without these qualities, Anderson thinks, great problems cannot be resolved.

\*      \*      \*

....People, people, people. They hurry to work, or return home, hasten to the college, take the youngsters to an infant-care center, come from the department store, chat with someone, see their dear ones, relatives, and friends off on a train, meet someone. What kind of people did they become under conditions of real Socialism? If you go for a journey on the Trans-Siberian Railroad, you will have quite a few interesting meetings, conversations, and observations.

You will find out that, if several decades ago the main occupations in Siberia were those of hunter, fisherman, lumberjack, gold prospector, and deer breeder, the economic portrait of the region has undergone a transformation. The scientist, construction worker, oil worker, miner, metallurgist, power plant technician, industrial chemist, teacher, physician, and movie projectionist—it is precisely their labor which today ushers in a new stage in the economic growth of the eastern districts of the U.S.S.R., the stage of overall mastery of the natural wealth and development of industry. Siberia and the Far East play an ever-expanding part in the economy of the country. In the opinion of experts, the economic importance of Siberia will go beyond the limits of the continent and acquire a global significance.

357

# *Appendix*

## Table 1.
### Population Growth of Siberian Cities
### (1000 People)

| City | 1939 | 1959 | 1977 |
|---|---|---|---|
| Novosibirsk | 404 | 885 | 1304 |
| Sverdlovsk | 423 | 779 | 1187 |
| Omsk | 289 | 581 | 1026 |
| Krasnoyarsk | 190 | 412 | 769 |
| Vladivostok | 206 | 291 | 536 |
| Khabarovsk | 207 | 323 | 524 |
| Tomsk | 145 | 249 | 423 |
| Tyumen | 79 | 150 | 347 |
| Ulan Ude | 126 | 174 | 308 |
| Chita | 121 | 172 | 294 |
| Abakan | 37 | 56 | 123 |
| Angarsk | — | 135 | 233 |
| Bratsk | — | 43 | 203 |
| Komsomolsk-on-the-Amur | 71 | 177 | 252 |
| Nakhodka | — | 64 | 129 |
| Surgut | — | 6 | 74 |
| Ust-Ilimsk | — | 21 [1970] | 53 |
| Yakutsk | 53 | 74 | 149 |

## Table 2
### Distance of Some Siberian Cities from Moscow (Including Soviet Far East)

| | |
|---|---|
| Sverdlovsk | 1667 km |
| Bratsk | 5000 km |
| Yakutsk | 8468 km |
| Anadyr | 11,091 km |
| Petropavlovsk-Kamchatsky | 11,876 km |

## Table 3
### Economic Advances of Siberia and the Far East

| Item | 1965 | 1976 |
|---|---|---|
| Electric power (billion kwh) | 30 | 82 |
| Natural gas (billion m³) | 1.4 | 72 |
| Lumber (million m³) | 42 | 74 |
| Tinned fish (million tins) | 187 | 559 |

## Table 4
## Production of Timber (million m³)

| Area | 1940 | 1965 | 1976 |
|------|------|------|------|
| Urals | 4 | 13 | 13 |
| Western Siberia | 3 | 8 | 9 |
| Eastern Siberia | 3 | 15 | 17 |
| Far East | 3 | 6 | 7 |

## Table 5
## Production of Oil and Natural Gas in Siberia

| | Oil (million tons) | | Gas (billion m³) | |
|------|--------|---------|--------|---------|
| | U.S.S.R. | Siberia | U.S.S.R. | Siberia |
| 1980 Plan | 620-640 | 315 | 400-435 | 155 |

V. Kuranov

## Table 6
## *Largest Rivers of Siberia and the Far East*

| Russian Federation | Length (in km) | Area (1000 m²) |
|---|---|---|
| *Western Siberia* | | |
| Ob | 5410 | 2975 |
| Irtysh | 4248 | 1643 |
| Ishim | 2450 | 177 |
| Chulym | 1799 | 134 |
| Ket | 1621 | 94.2 |
| Tobol | 1591 | 405 |
| *Eastern Siberia* | | |
| Yenisey | 4092 | 2580 |
| Selenga | 1480 | 447 |
| Bargusin | 416 | 20 |
| Upper Angara | 452 | 22 |
| *Far East* | | |
| Amur | 2846 | 995 |
| Kolyma | 2600 | 644 |
| Zeya | 1242 | 233 |
| Anadyr | 1145 | 191 |
| Omolon | 1100 | 118.6 |

## Table 7
## Number of Physicians in Siberia and the Far East
## (per 1000 people)

| Area | 1941 | 1966 | 1977 |
|---|---|---|---|
| Western Siberia | 5 | 25 | 41 |
| Eastern Siberia | 3 | 14 | 24 |
| Far East | 3 | 15 | 25 |

# Index

Page numbers in italic refer to photographs.

# Index

# Index

# Index